Why Smart People Make Dumb Mistakes With Their Money

T0161743

Why Smart People Make Dumb Mistakes With Their Money

Kerry Johnson, MBA, Ph.D.

MEDIA

Published 2019 by Gildan Media LLC
aka G&D Media
www.GandDmedia.com

FIRST EDITION 2019

Front Cover design by David Rheinhardt of Pyrographx

Interior design by Meghan Day Healey of Story Horse, LLC

Library of Congress Cataloging-in-Publication Data is available upon request

ISBN: 978-1-7225-0197-6

10   9   8   7   6   5   4   3   2   1

To my tennis buddies,
Mark, Peter, Paul, Keith, Denny, Scott, Les,
my brother Kevin and his wife Sharon,
as well many others who told me
hair raising stories of investments gone bad
and the frustrations of making
the right money decisions.

Contents

Introduction

A s recently as 15 years ago, economists thought investors were essentially logical and rational. They were assumed to generally act in their own best interest.

They made decisions to minimize risk and maximize return. They tried to protect the family and focus on future needs. But now we know that people are ruled by their emotions, moods, and biases. As in any new field, behavioral economists started to notice strange facts and odd observations standard economists could not explain. For example, why do gamblers keep betting even when on a losing streak? Why do people make New Year's resolutions with the best of intentions, and then quickly go back to their old bad habits, no matter how self-sabotaging? Some people even exact revenge on others who've wronged them, even when that behavior is self-destructive.

In one example of behavioral economics, a manufacturer wanted to get rid of a line of soap to make room for a new product. The economists on the company staff simply told the execs to charge less for the soap they wanted to eliminate. Yet behavioral economists advised that simply displaying the soap at eye level would cause buyers to notice it first. They took the advice of the behaviorists and the soap sold out quickly.

Bounded Rationality

In the 1940s, Herbert Simon of Carnegie Mellon University and also a Nobel Prize winner put forth the idea of "Bounded Rationality." He argued rational thought alone did not explain human decision-making. The surprise was Simon was not even an economist, which probably explained his fresh thinking.

In the beginning, economists thought that Bounded Rationality or behavioral irrationality (a more accurate label) could not be true, because even if there are illogical, irrational people around, they will still have to compete with smart, rational, experienced investors who will take the assets of the less intelligent.

For example, if investors become illogical about GE and dump the shares on the market, smart investors would step in and buy the undervalued stock, turning a tidy profit. But this logical approach was not always the case. In fact, Royal Dutch Petroleum sold at a different price in Amsterdam than shares of Shell were selling for in London, even though they were shares of the same company, Royal Dutch Shell. You would think that a logical investor would know the difference.

But Bounded Rationality won out.

In one study by Harvard researcher Sendhil Mullainathan, 70,000 letters were sent to previous bank borrowers, "Congratulations, you're eligible for a special interest rate!" But the offer was randomized. Some got a lower rate, others a higher one. Aspects of the letters were also randomized. Some letters included a photo of a bank employee varied by gender and race.

Also different types of graphic tables were displayed differing in complexity of the types of loans offered.

Some letters pitched a chance to win a cell phone for a new account and some had deadlines. The researchers discovered any one of these variables had the effect of dropping the loan interest rate of 1%–5%. A woman's photo increased loan demand among men as much as did dropping the interest rate by 5%. And the loan sizes weren't insignificant; we are talking about big loans here. Often the payments were up to 10% of the borrower's income. The study showed the interest rate was only the third most important reason for purchasing the loans.

When you see economic data projections from mainstream economists, they assume people act logically, rationally, and behave in their own self-interest.

They assume people will weigh the costs of their own decisions depending on the level of profit and value.

But the perfect human beings economists create models for do not exist. Actually, you and I are irrational, self-sabotaging, and sometimes even self-sacrificing.

So behavioral economics and behavioral investing is really the explanation of how people make choices and invest their money often directed by their own passionate, emotional purposes.

My daughter Caroline, at age 17, got her first job working at a boutique. She was thrilled with the job even though she was only making minimum wage. She was required to work either as a volunteer or in a paid position, but couldn't spend the summer sitting around. I even sweetened the pot by offering to pay a 25% allowance bonus as an incentive. I even got her a debit card linked to her checking account. But she may lose the job before the school year started and could only spend about 25% of her salary. After three months of working, I checked her bank account and noticed she spent every penny. Now, we expect that from a 17-year-old kid, but we don't expect this self-destructive financial behavior from an adult. Surprisingly, this is the kind of behavior nearly all of us exhibit at some point. In the rest of this book, you will discover examples of your own biases and irrational craziness.

You will learn what these behaviors are and how to avoid them. Part of learning how to deal with these strange behaviors is to first recognize them and then stop you from the self-sabotage.

ONE
Mental Accounting

People who exhibit "Mental Accounting" rationalize that money won is in a different bucket than money earned. They can spend it differently and use it with more abandon. The truth is no matter how the money comes to you whether earned, given, or invested, it is worth the same. People tend to pigeonhole

> *"I just won this money so I think I'll just blow it all"*

money into separate self-contained accounts and categories.

This allows them to be more risky or conservative, depending on where they put it.

Once in a while, a financial advisor will outline to a prospective client their losses by using another broker.

Sometimes the client will explain away the losses by saying, "It's all paper money anyway," suggesting it's not real. This is a good example of Mental Accounting.

People don't really think they own or possess money unless it's in a bank account or green in their pocket.

Mental Accounting can be useful because it helps us treat savings for college and retirement as different buckets of money than the cash we use for casual spending. But it causes problems when you receive money from sources like salary, bonuses, gifts, or tax refunds. Those monies are spent differently and more quickly than money earned. I remember one client who had a savings account. They wouldn't spend that sacrosanct money, no matter what the need. The money could be used for college, past due mortgages, or even a non life-threatening emergency. But they were so nervous they would run out of money, it became a type of lock box never to be opened, even in the direst of circumstances. Contrast this to another situation in which a client thinks whenever an account earns interest, it is their money to spend. If you feel the need to have "mad money," just take 5% of your income and put it into a different account. This will help you spend money in an organized way instead of the money that burns a hole in your pocket when you feel rich.

When Mental Accounting works, it keeps investors from raiding their retirement accounts to spend frivolously.

Many did this with their home equity loans before the "Great Recession" of 2008. An example of this might be a 529 college education fund. You wouldn't think of raiding a college account unless you were about to lose your house. After all, this is the bucket of money allowing your kids to go to college.

I remember back in the 1970s when I was playing professional tennis, my mother gave me her VW camper van as a college graduation present. I was leaving for Europe for a couple of years, so I sold the van for $3,000 and put the money in a bank account in case I had a lean time on the tour. I wasn't a world class player, so having a "lean time" was a probability.

It wasn't exactly Cortez's "burn the ships" commitment, but at least I would have a cushion. This was my bucket of money allowing me to play tennis and get me through the weeks when I would lose in the first round. But apparently my mother thought the $3,000 was her own spendable bucket of money.

After losing in the first round of three tournaments, I called my mom asking for the money to be wired to Germany. She didn't have it anymore and apologized.

As it turned out, this was the best thing for me. Just like Cortez, I had to either win or hitchhike and swim back to California from Europe. Of course I don't fault my mom. She probably needed it more than me. But as a result, I became very resourceful and earned enough for the rest of my tour. There were no millions in winnings or endorsements, but I did make it from tournament to tournament.

Let's assume you had a ticket to the World Series, or at least a hard to get ticket to a show. At the venue, you realize the $250 ticket has disappeared. Would you buy another ticket using a credit card? Would you rationalize since you are already there, you might as well just spend the money for another ticket? Here's another scenario for you. Let's assume you reserved a ticket at the box office, but lost the $250 in cash on the way to the event. Would you be more likely to go home in this situation, or still spend the $250?

Many people say they would cough up the $250 to replace the vanished ticket quicker than they would spend another $250 to cover the lost cash. Again, this is an example of Mental Accounting.

Mental Accounting may also keep you from becoming wealthy. Many just can't seem to save up enough to invest for retirement. They're usually cost conscious when making large purchase like cars and houses. But when it comes to small purchases, they lose discipline. I was in Vail, Colorado recently and stopped to get gas for a rental car. As soon as I drove by the pump, I discovered gas was $0.30 more per gallon than at the station I just passed one exit earlier. I pulled away from the station and told my daughter it was too expensive and that I was going to drive back to the other station. She then said, "What? Why are you trying to save only a dollar?" But unless I'm spending a dollar to save a dollar, avoiding spending more than necessary will, in time, prevent that dollar from being invested. This is also a form of Mental Accounting.

"If you give me a dollar, I will spend two"

So if you spend a dollar or $100 several times a day rather than saving it, your investments will be impacted, and also, in time, the security of your retirement.

You might be thinking, "It depends on how wealthy you are!" Yet the more money you have, the more likely you are to make these kinds of mistakes. It just occurs on a bigger scale.

Marginal Propensity to Consume

Economists call "Marginal Propensity to Consume" the theory explaining why some people cannot accumulate enough money to become wealthy or retire comfortably. Marginal Propensity to Consume (MPC) is defined as the percentage of an incremental dollar you spend rather than save. So if you receive a $200 tax refund and spend $160, your spending rate is 0.80 or 80%. But if all you do is spend money given to you, things may not be so bad. Many years ago, an economist at the Bank of Israel conducted a study of Israelis who were given restitution payments from the post-World War

II Government of Germany. The money was intended to make up for Nazi atrocities against the Jews. But the payments could also be described as Mental Accounting "found money" to the recipients.

The payments varied in size from family to family and individual to individual. The restitution was often equal to two-thirds of the recipient's annual income.

In this group, many had a spending rate of 23%. So that for every dollar received, 23% more was spent.

But the group that received the smallest payments of about 7% had a spending rate of 200%. So for every dollar they received, they spent two dollars. You might say for every dollar of found money, they spent another dollar from income or savings. This happened to me when I played tennis in Europe. I just won the second round in St. Moritz, Switzerland, and made a whopping $150. I immediately put the money in the bank. But then one of the fans offered to pay me $100 for a one-hour lesson, sort of like $300 in today's dollars. So that hundred dollars became found money. I took my friends and their girlfriends out for drinks at an expensive Swiss restaurant. As you might imagine, I spent $100 on drinks, but then another $100 on dinner rationalizing that it was a rare occasion that probably wouldn't happen again. So my Marginal Propensity to Consume number was 2 (200%). If I had kept making that mistake throughout my life, it would be difficult to save any money at all.

One of the best examples of Mental Accounting was a PBS special on how people save money. There were about six people in the group interviewed by a PBS host. At one point, the host asked how many owned savings accounts. She then asked how many also had credit card balances. I was shocked. Not only did all six have savings accounts, but they also admitted to credit card balances drawing an 18% interest rate. The host then asked one participant why she had a savings account in addition to credit card debt. She could just use the savings to pay off the credit card and avoid interest entirely. The guest replied she wanted to have an emergency fund in case something terrible happened. This is an example of how some people are tied to credit cards and often unable to get out of debt.

You are a victim of Mental Accounting if you have emergency funds, yet still have credit card debt. You are a victim of Mental Accounting if you have trouble saving, but don't think to recognize you are reckless spender. You are a victim of Mental Accounting if you're more likely to spend a tax refund than funds from your savings account. You are a victim of Mental Accounting if you don't look at money you invest with the same rigor as money you earn.

One famous example of Mental Accounting is from research done by a behavioral economics researcher named Camerer in a study of New York City cab drivers.

The cab drivers were paid a flat cab rental for 24 hours. Any money they earned would be profit after the fee. Each driver could decide how long or how little to work each day. One strategy would be to work longer on the good days, such as rain or convention days; or quit early on the bad days. What Camerer found was each cab driver set a target earnings amount for the good days. When they met that amount, the drivers would quit. When the bad days came, the drivers tended to work longer hours to make up for the limited earnings on the good days. This is totally irrational behavior. Yet think of a sales rep making two sales on one day and then going home. But on the days without sales, he works late into the night. Mental Accounting is prevalent in other areas besides how you spend money. It often dictates how you work.

TWO
Fungibility

One of the key concepts of Mental Accounting is "Fungibility." This concept holds that all dollars should be worth the same. Whether you win $100 on the slot machines, $100 in salary, or receive a $100 tax refund check, it should all spend the same. One hundred dollars in your wallet should create the same level of financial wellbeing as $100 in your savings account.

One of my mentors, John Savage, worked with high net worth individuals. John would put these affluent clients into life insurance vehicles as *"I only lost money on paper"* a way of protecting their wealth. One day speaking at a seminar, he admitted one client had $1 Million in a mattress which he moved to a life insurance policy. Then he got a question from an attendee asking why he put his client's $1 million into a life insurance contract. "Why not put the money into a mix of mutual funds, bonds and other investments?" John metaphorically said, "You are laughing at why someone would have $1 million in a mattress when they could make a lot more in riskier investments? My question to you is, "How much money do you have in your mattress right now?"

John was simply making the point it's not that people invest poorly, but that most people just don't save enough to invest in all. John also stressed that keeping money safe is more important than where it is invested.

I'm sure the million-dollar client felt as wealthy with the money in a mattress as he did in a life insurance contract, and probably a lot safer.

THREE
Status Quo Bias

People tend to stay with the investments they have no matter what the performance. I coach many financial advisors and brokers who work with prospective clients who refuse to change brokers. Often the brokers are churning (frequently trading) while charging high fees.

They may even lose money in supposedly safe accounts, often putting their clients at financial risk. My clients usually explain to the prospective clients how they are losing money and may be getting ripped off. Yet an investor often says things like, "I've been with my broker for ten years, I think I would feel uncomfortable if I left now."

This is totally illogical behavior. The client is not working for the broker, the broker supposedly is being paid "I can't change that now, it just doesn't feel right" for performance by the investor. Yet the investor can't break the bond because of a desire to preserve the status quo.

In another case, one of my clients held an investor seminar at a very prestigious country club. He spent an hour talking to the attendees about how to convert retirement accounts into safe investments that can never lose money. 80% of the families booked appointments.

Nearly all of them met with my client to talk about how investments like annuities could help them avoid further losses. When one couple heard the details of the annuity, they cancelled the next appointment.

My coaching client eventually was able to reach them by telephone. They admitted telling their broker about the annuity who then presented it himself. This is irrational.

Why would an investor choose to stay with a broker who didn't offer the annuity long ago? This couple had no contact with their broker for two years.

Yet they felt obligated to treat the broker much better than he treated them.

There was a very interesting television commercial recently depicting a fat cat broker trying to convince his client why they should not leave his firm. During a Scott Trade commercial, the broker hypocritically tells the client how much the relationship means while the broker is sitting in the back of a limousine reading a magazine during the phone call. Now you and I both know this commercial is hyperbole. Yet a broker who doesn't keep in contact also doesn't deserve to keep their book of business. Some clients are so worried about losing what they have; they avoid taking the risk to get something better. This is a good example of Status Quo Bias.

You are probably a victim of Status Quo Bias if you tend to disregard new ideas, dismiss concepts that may cause change, and feel locked into your own habits. It's difficult for anyone to change. But Status Quo Bias victims want to stay where they are often in spite of the consequences. You have gleaned throughout this program that I play a lot of tennis. I have been playing competitively since I was four years old. A few years ago, I kept my head tennis racket for two years past the time that I should've trashed it. It caused severe tennis elbow, but I resisted the change. This is an example of irrational behavior that kept me in pain. A rational person would have purchased a new racket.

An irrational person would have avoided making a change.

In one study of Status Quo Bias, William Samuelson of Boston University gave students a choice between four investments. One stock had a 50% chance of staying the same, another 40% chance, a bond with a 9% return, and a municipal bond with a 6% tax free return. The students were asked which one they wanted to pick. Some chose a bond, some chose a stock. Yet after the choice was made, they were informed they already owned one of the previous choices. 47% chose to stay with the investment already in their portfolio than stick with the choice they made. 30% of students chose the municipal bond. Yet when they were told they already owned the muni, nearly half thought muni-bonds were the way to go. This is a good example when what you own in your portfolio holds more value than anything else presented.

It's one thing to recognize decisions are often based on Status Quo Bias, but another knowing how to cure yourself of this irrational decision-making behavior.

Simply ask yourself if you would buy the same investment again. If the answer is no, you should sell it immediately.

If the answer is yes, you have a reason for the investment being properly apportioned in your portfolio. This is a good rule of thumb in evaluating any asset or any investment you currently own. Just ask yourself if you would buy it again. If no, sell it now.

FOUR
Endowment Effect

A nother area of behavioral investing is the "Endowment Effect." This concept indicates "what's mine is valuable and what's yours isn't." This theory partly explains Status Quo Bias. In other words, what I have is more valuable than what you are presenting to me. In one study from behavioral economist Richard Thaler, economics students at Cornell University were given mugs free of charge to sell with a suggested price of $6. The interesting part was they were allowed to sell the mugs for whatever price they could *"Leggo of my eggo"* get. But keep in mind the mugs were given to them without cost. Something interesting occurred in the sales process. The price the students were unwilling to sell below was $5.25. The price students were unwilling to pay above was only $2.75. No sale! Since the value of an item is only what people are willing to pay, the mugs were valued much more highly by the students selling them than the students who wanted to buy.

This is also an example of why garage sale negotiations can be difficult. For example, you might struggle to price your favorite wingback chair. This is the chair you bought for $500 ten years ago, read books to your young kids in, sometimes even took naps in, and almost a member of your family. Think of the sitcom "Fraser" with the father who wouldn't part with his beat up, broken down, favorite chair. Because of the history with the chair, you attach a price tag of $250. But the possible buyer offers only $35.

You are insulted and slightly angry. "These buyers can't recognize the value of your family heirloom." The endowment effect has set in. It's difficult to part with something possessing so much emotional history.

Even though you don't feel emotionally fond of investments the same way you would a chair, bed, or even a home, once you take ownership, your emotional connection may make it worth more than a buyer wants to pay.

The endowment effect may also have an impact on your chance to become wealthy. Many of us pay too much attention to our out-of-pocket expenses and not enough on how much investments may be worth in the future. In one study by Bucks Consultants, only 50% of those eligible to contribute to their 401(k) pension funds took advantage of it, even when contributions were matched by their employer. Parting with money was viewed as an out-of-pocket expense (Endowment Effect). "If I put $10,000 in a pension fund, I won't be able to afford my new car this year."

Forget about the substantially better Porsche you will be able to buy in 20 years by investing. The notion here is "money I have today is more valuable than the greater amount I could earn later by investing over the next 20 years."

Dan Ariely, in his book Predictably Irrational, makes the point that one man's ceiling is another man's floor. If you're the owner, you're at the ceiling and when you're the buyer, you're the floor. A very popular TV program called "Antiques Road Show" is a good example of Endowment Effect. The stereotype is of someone who buys a painting for $10 which turns out to be a Rembrandt worth hundreds of thousands.

More frequently, an owner brings in an heirloom desk handed down from a great-grandfather that turns out to be worth only $50. Of course, we never see those owners on the TV show arguing the desk is worth more than the appraiser suggests. What we do see is the shocked and startled owner who didn't know the amazing value sitting in their attic for the last 50 years.

Ariely tells the story of students camping out for days at Duke University trying to get valuable Duke Basketball March Madness finals tickets. Those who camped out for up to a week were willing to sell the tickets for $2,400. Those who did not camp out were only willing to pay $170. After all, the sellers invested sweat and sleepless nights to get the tickets.

The Endowment Effect may also have an impact on what part of your portfolio you are married to and what you are willing to sell. One of my coaching clients mentioned his financial planning client who owned more than $1 million of stock. The investor owned GM stock for more than 20 years yet lost money for the last five. When the adviser told the investor it was time to sell, he was very resistant. Later he admitted his father and grandfather worked for GM. He felt very loyal to the company. Yet this lack of understanding about the Endowment Effect caused the investor to consistently lose money pushing his retirement date more years away than he hoped for.

Here's another example. Mr. Smith recently visited a financial adviser to evaluate his current investment holdings. He had a long-term CD valued at $600,000, 1,200 shares of IBM valued at $130,000, and 3,000 shares of GE with a stock value of $65,000. Mr. Smith was in his early 50's and had no intention of retiring soon. He wanted his assets to grow and had no immediate income needs.

His retirement time horizon was 20 years. His goal was to leave money to his daughter when he passed. The financial adviser told Mr. Smith to allocate at least two-thirds of his assets to a broadly diversified portfolio of stocks that included international equities as well as corporate bonds instead of just CDs. This would give him a higher yield. But the advisor did not know that Mr. Smith inherited the investments from his father and were the only securities he ever owned. Even though Mr. Smith could have made changes to his portfolio without tax consequences, he chose to stay with what he had. This is a real life example of how the Endowment Effect can prevent you from making good investment choices.

One way to avoid the deleterious impact of Endowment Effect is to look at your portfolio and decide if you are emotionally attached to the investments in it.

Are you married to GM? Are you married to the idea of owning gold because your parents swore by it, even though the lack of diversity creates a lower rate of return?

If you have owned IBM for 20 years, do you feel attached? This is the same logic as if you had that old wingback chair from 15 years ago. How much would you pay for that chair if it didn't have an emotional connection?

Recognizing the Endowment Effect will allow you to set a price in a garage sale that people are willing to pay. Knowing about this effect will also help you make correct decisions about appropriate assets in your portfolio.

FIVE
Foot in the Door

One interesting concept of the Endowment Effect is the "Foot in the Door theory." If a marketer can get you to take something home, it's unlikely you will return it. Whatever the value, it will increase if you take possession of it. When I first got married, I had a misguided illusion my wife wanted a vacuum cleaner for her birthday. My sweet wife saw the vacuum and just smiled. Looking back, I can't believe I did something so stupid.

What she really wanted were diamonds, chocolates, and flowers. But I saw the Hoover in a mall and walked in. The salesman showed me a heavy metal bullet and flipped the vacuum on sucking it through 30 feet of hose. He then looked at me and said, "Don't make your decision now. Just take it home for a week and bring it back if you don't think it's the best vacuum you have ever owned." So I gave him a credit

"Try it, you'll like it"

card and took the cleaner home fully expecting to return it within a week. A month later I saw the vacuum in the kitchen and wondered when I actually made the decision to buy.

One of my CD programs, "Peak Performance," offers a guarantee to increase sales by 80% within eight weeks. This program out-sells all my other CDs 3:1.

I even advertise if the listener does not increase their sales by at least 80% within eight weeks, they can return it for a refund. I rarely get this title back. The truth of the matter is if any CD buyer returns a program, we will refund the money gladly. It happens so infrequently. My brother Kevin owns a video distribution company in Redlands, California. He sells business training videos with the offer that the buyer only pays the shipping costs. They can keep it for one month. But if they don't get the video back in 30 days, their credit card will be hit with $99. Since the videos are subscription-based, most buyers don't return anything until the fourth month.

Another aspect of "Foot in the Door" theory is our tendency to stick with initial impressions. The father of comparative psychology, Konrad Lorenz, called this phenomenon, "Imprinting." For example, say you make a political statement at a party. Someone then confronts you with another view, perhaps more logical.

You may find yourself defending your stance. Your wife comes home with a new dress and brags about the great deal she got. You mention seeing the exact dress $10 cheaper at another store. She defends her purchase that it's better quality than the cheaper one you saw. Sometimes "Foot in the Door" theory should be called "foot in the mouth." You make a poorly thought out statement, yet won't admit your mistake until it's too late. You decide to buy an investment only to watch it lose value soon after. Then you defend the choice rationalizing it will come back in value.

One other example of "Foot in the Door" theory is what I call the "eBay effect." You make a bid for a very cool golf putter. The next day, you go back to the site only to discover someone outbid you by $5.

You start thinking about the strokes the putter will save on your next round. You can feel the putter in your hands and, in a sense, you already own it. You go back to the site and bid $5 more. After two or three more rounds of this bidding, you finally win. But the win was costly. You spent $25 more for the putter that it was listed for at the local golf store. This virtual ownership cost you some money.

This is a big reason why many companies offer trial promotions. Credit card companies advertise zero interest for 30 days, a health club offers a 75% discount for the first month, and even DirecTV presents premium movie channels free for the first year. Now no one ever expects to pay for these channels longer than the free period. DirecTV knows you will keep those expensive premium channels for years after the discount time expires.

"People will be more disappointed by the things they didn't do than the things they did." —Mark Twain

I pay a monthly fee of $79 for a teleconference site. The company originally offered a premium service free for 90 days. The fee would then go up from $59 to $79 a month. That was three years ago.

I'm still paying $79. What all these companies have in common is their ability to create ownership before you buy.

Some insurance companies offer a free look. Many give you ten days to rescind your purchase. This almost never happens. Car companies like Hyundai advertise a month to return the car if you don't like it. Almost nobody does. This is a pretty easy sales ploy since all they have to do is make the offer. It seems risk free.

Not really. The choice to buy was made when you drove off the lot on a "trial basis."

SIX

Loss Aversion

Most investors are more worried about losing money than motivated to make it. In tennis, we often tell ourselves losing feels worse than the joy of winning. In fact many would rather not take a risk at all if there is a chance of failing. This is one of the reasons why entrepreneurs are so very well-paid and so very few. Not many are willing to risk everything they own for one chance in 20 of success. A symptom of Loss Aversion is trading too soon when the market loses value or worse yet, failing to invest at all.

In 1994, University of Michigan professor Nejat Seyhun discovered if an investor missed the 40 best performing days of the market within a 30 year period, their average annual return would have dropped from 12% to 7%. One test to see if you are affected by Loss Aversion is whether you would be tempted

> *"I am totally willing to gamble if there is no way I can lose"*

to take all or some of your money out if the market dips by 25%, assuming you don't need it immediately. Conversely, when the market is bullish, would you be willing to take your money out if it becomes overvalued. One of my clients, Peter Kohli, has a client with EE Bonds.

The bonds only pay between 1 and 2% return, actually losing money after inflation. But at least they're safe.

The fear of regret (changing status quo) is actually stronger than the desire to take a risk for a future benefit.

Sam Walton of Wal-Mart fame once said the biggest regret in one's twilight years is not making mistakes or taking too much risk; it is taking too little risk.

Richard Thaler, once wrote in the "Journal of Economic Behavior and Organization," more people make mistakes by not investing at all than investing poorly.

Mark Twain once said that more people will be disappointed by the things they didn't do than the things they did. The reality is people experience intense regret for their mistakes in the short-term. But not taking risks over the long-term is much more painful. It is sort of what I don't know, I don't know.

I live in Orange County, close to Hollywood. One of the things I love about starving actors is they are taking a risk. Perhaps not taking a risk long enough to succeed, but at least they are going for it. The same is true for entrepreneurs. Most of us can't stomach that much risk. Yet there is more job safety working for yourself than being employed by someone else. A decrease in income is better than losing your job and having no income.

Suppose you own $1,000 worth of stock in GE.

A friend suggested you sell it and buy $1,000 worth of IBM. But you decide not to take your friend's advice and GE stock drops

30% turning your $1,000 into $700. Here is another scenario. Suppose you own $1,000 of GE stock. A friend suggests that you sell GE and put $1,000 into IBM. You take the suggestion and move your money. But then IBM drops 30% causing your $1,000 to decrease to $700.

Which scenario would make you feel worse? Not taking your friend's advice and staying with GE dropping 30%, or taking your friend's advice and moving the money into IBM only to watch it decrease 30% from $1,000 down to $700. Chances are you would be unhappier moving the money than taking no action at all. There's no doubt both situations would be unpleasant, but the regret of making the wrong decision, if it turns out poorly, would be more painful than making no decision at all.

I have often kicked myself for making decisions that don't work out. But whether it's a decision for an investment or business, most of us will avoid regret by taking no action all.

One of my favorite life lessons is airline travel. My joke is that I fly 8,000 miles a week which is nothing if you know how far my bags travel. About one-third of my flights are delayed or cancelled, and it's getting worse.

The most risky period to fly is during thunderstorm season in the Spring and Summer. When one flight gets delayed, it cascades throughout the airlines' whole system. Sometimes I will ask a gate agent to hold my connection while I run to it. They will usually caution me not to try advising I won't make it. Yet I almost always do. I have learned that taking small daily risks prepares one for the bigger, more calculated risks later.

One way to overcome Loss Aversion is to decide in advance to make a decision. If the market is going down, you may be tempted to sell your investments.

Research what your next step might be, but either way, make a decision. George W. Bush was second guessed after his presidency about the premise of invading Iraq.

But he never wavered from his decision to commit troops based on the information he had at the time.

Be able to defend later your options and that you made the right decision at the time. But be able to cite the reasons why. If it works great or if it doesn't, you learned something. It's unlikely you will make consistently bad decisions. Taking a risk on balance is a net benefit, because if you made a mistake, you also learned to avoid the same mistake again. It has been said that Edison tried 10,000 variations of the light bulb before he found one that worked.

I played a tennis tournament a few years ago against a player with an awesome forehand. I've got a pretty big serve and in the second set found myself in a tie breaker. I was serving for the match and took aim at his backhand. As I hit the ball, my opponent unexpectedly stepped to his left and nailed the return down the line for a winner. He also won the next point and then the match. I was really mad at myself for serving to the wrong spot. But during most of the match, his backhand seemed much weaker. Sure it bothered me, but with the information I had, it was the right decision to make. He just got lucky and won the match.

SEVEN
Number Numbness

Tom Brady, then quarterback for the New England Patriots was being interviewed on ESPN a few years ago. The host asked Tom about his game plan against the San Diego Chargers.

Tom said he was going to give 150%. You and I both know that 100% is the max you can give. Apparently Tom Brady can contribute more than the rest of us. Baseball great Yogi Berra once said, "A nickel isn't worth a dime anymore." But my favorite Yogi line is, "Half the lies they tell about me aren't true."

> *"Half the lies they tell about me aren't true"*
> *—Yogi Berra*

These are all examples of "Number Numbness."

An investor called his financial adviser one day to complain about a $4,000 loss. The adviser mentioned the decrease was indeed $4,000. But the portfolio totaled more than $2 million. The investor was blind to the overall performance and the small loss in relation to the portfolio. He only focused on the small dent in his account.

Much of Number Numbness is the inability of an investor to recognize the impact of inflation and the present value of money. For example, a person who invests $10,000 today in the stock market could make nearly $67,020 over a couple of decades assuming a 10% average annual return. But someone who invests $10,000 in U.S. treasury bonds earning a 6% return, will have about $32,000. Many people will gladly give up the stock market risk and go for the treasury bonds netting $32,000 than deal with the volatility and risk of the stock market even though it could possibly result in $67,000.

Recently, I bought a product on eBay for $21, seven dollars less than any other vendor. But once I checked out of the transaction, I noticed the shipping cost was twice as much with the $21 vendor than a competing $28 vendor. The more expensive $28 seller was actually less expensive than the lower cost choice. If someone bought the $21 product, they would be a Number Numbness victim. Another example of Number Numbness is government expenditures.

> *"Six of one, half dozen of the other"*

In 2009, the US Congress approved an $800 Billion government stimulus package. We also heard that a city manager in Bell, California received an $800,000 salary. But we are so jaded today by the media debt reports; even an $800K city manager salary doesn't shock us. Yet even a $1.4 trillion deficit means that every man, woman, and child in America owes $121,000. Strangely, that doesn't cause riots in the streets because the numbers we hear everyday amount to information overload. Numbers now fail to shock us.

I stopped by a Shell gas station in Orange, California.

The sign in front of the station advertised $3.13 per gallon. I filled my tank and realized I had paid $3.50 per gallon for 20 gallons and wondered what happened. I noticed a sign on the left mentioning a car wash with a tank fill up would be only $3.13 per gallon. Of course, to get the $3.13 per gallon, you had to spend $9 for the car wash. I can make the case that I just didn't pay attention, yet I chose to only look at the lower price number on the sign instead of the whole thing. Again this is an example of Number Numbness.

Number Numbness can cost you the most money with day to day purchases. Most of us routinely ignore the rate we pay for insurance whether it's homeowner's, health, auto, or even life. We just compare prices between companies. Often we evaluate low deductibles assuming a claim won't cost more than $500 out of pocket. Yet the chances of an expensive car repair, a fire in your house or even a catastrophic health problem is fairly remote. But here comes the Number Numbness.

If your car insurance deductible is $500, your premiums overall will be 25% higher than with a deductible of $1000.

Years ago, the NBA LA Lakers' guard Derek Fisher shot a season average of 32%. Kobe Bryant's shooting average was 43% overall. But Derek had a hot hand during the NBA finals. In the final three seconds of the game, he was handed the ball trying to hit a three point shot. Derek dribbled past the defender, moved to a position with his toes slightly in back of the threepoint line, put the ball up and whiffed the rim. While it's easy to second guess the decision to give Fisher the ball, passing to Kobe in retrospect would have been much wiser. Kobe had a much higher overall shooting percentage for the year. Even though Derek was hot that night, the probability of making the game-winning shot was only as good as his overall shooting percentage for the year. Most mutual funds are chosen using exactly this "hot hand tonight" strategy. A study done by Columbia University professor, Noel

Capon found the single biggest reason people use to select mutual funds is recent performance. Yet past performance is a notoriously unreliable guide in predicting future results. 75% of mutual funds perform worse than the underlying index. Last year's star may be this year's goat.

Surprisingly, in one study conducted by Northwestern Mutual Life Insurance, Americans showed understanding of diversification, asset allocation and dollar-cost averaging, while flunking other basic questions.

Overall, the study implied that worries during the 2008 economic downturn did not lead Americans to learn more about personal finance.

A large majority—88%—could pick out the definition of diversification and 79% correctly answered a question about asset allocation. Fifty-seven percent correctly chose a definition of dollar-cost-averaging.

But on other questions, respondents were largely ignorant.

For example, only 35% of respondents knew that the average rate of inflation in one 2010 study was closer to 3% than 6% or 9%.

Half of those tested responded incorrectly that bonds offer better protection from inflation than stocks. Only 32% knew that index funds seek to match the returns of stock or bond benchmarks. Few respondents showed basic understanding of insurance products.

Only 27% knew that permanent life insurance can pay dividends. Nearly half believed incorrectly that term life insurance is more likely to have cash value than permanent life insurance.

Dave Simbro, a Northwestern Mutual vice president, suggested that Americans understood the questions about diversification, asset allocation and dollar-cost averaging because those terms are used in company 401(k) materials. "But there's a mismatch between awareness and the ability to implement the concepts," he said. "And there's a big gap in understanding what life insurance can provide."

The study did find that people want to learn more in order to manage their economic circumstances.

When asked to rank the importance of understanding their own personal finances, nearly eight of ten respondents (79%) gave it a seven or above on a scale of one ("what I don't know won't hurt me") to ten ("I feel the need to know all I can about my financial situation").

Another symptom of Number Numbness is ignoring commission and fees. The average expense for a well diversified US stock mutual fund is 1.41%. Yet some funds charge an expense ratio of 3%. While this difference seems small, after ten years a 7% gain with a $10,000 investment would mean the difference between making $35,760 and $30,810.

Albert Einstein once said that compound interest is the eighth wonder of the world. Compounding means principal and interest this year will be used as a basis for next year. For example, if I make 20% on a $100 investment this year, it will be worth $120 by the end of the year. If I make the same interest next year, my $120 will be worth $144. If I can get a vendor to compound more frequently, for example quarterly or monthly, my investment will increase even faster.

You may have Number Numbness if:
- You have low insurance deductibles.
- You chase hot mutual fund returns.
- You don't pay attention to inflation and taxes.
- You ignore commission costs and fees.

One way that you can inoculate yourself from the ravages of Number Numbness is to pay attention to the expenses and income you incur with each decision.

For example, you may want to do a "what if" spreadsheet to see the cost of each possible investment decision.

When I was in business school studying for my MBA, we worked on decision trees evaluating the monetary outcome from each possible decision. For example a purchase of $1,000 over five years would be a lot less expensive than paying $1,000 today because of inflation. A few minutes of homework and measuring the outcome of each decision, will in the end save you a lot of money. This actually is very simple.

Estimate the possible return of an investment decision; subtract expenses and inflation for each year.

This is your expected rate of return. Of course you can make it more complex. You can add Beta, the relative risk of the investment and Alpha, the relative performance of the fund against their peers. But this simple exercise will help you get a better idea of how well your investment will really perform.

EIGHT
Sunk Cost Fallacy

Have you heard you shouldn't throw good money after bad? This refers to the "Sunk Cost Fallacy." Politicians make mistakes of ignoring this concept, frequently spending more and more money on already bad projects. Many years ago, Tennessee Senator Jim Sasser tried to appropriate money for a Tennessee dam project that was already $5 billion over budget.

The argument to his Congressional Ways and Means Committee colleagues was billions had already been spent on the project. They couldn't cancel it because so much money had already been spent.

Sort of like a clunker you have owned for the last ten years, now costing $300 per month in repairs.

"I can't sell it now, I have to wait for it to recover."

Yet you can't get rid of it because you've sunk so much money into the car already. Soon, you will realize the car is a money pit and sell it for whatever you can get.

Or better yet, suppose that someone gave you a minivan.

You discovered it needed a $1,000 transmission.

Contrast that to a minivan you've spent $10,000 on in repairs so far. You also just discovered it needed a $1,000 transmission. Would you be more likely to spend $1,000 on a car that was just given to you, or on a car you already sunk money in? You are more likely to put more money into a car that you've already spent (sunk) money on than one you haven't.

I remember a movie many years ago with Tom Hanks called "The Money Pit." The newlywed couple bought a two story fixer upper thinking they could bring it into pristine shape. But after tens of thousands of dollars, not only was the money sunk, but also their marriage. The tragic part was their inability to stop spending, eventually forcing them into bankruptcy.

Now I'm sure that would never happen to you. You would never allow Sunk Cost to force you into destitution.

But if you don't cut your losses, you will lose money until you have none left to lose.

The Sunk Cost Fallacy concept is taught in most good MBA schools. Students learn an over-budget project with a diminished chance of return should be terminated. Yet even the best business minds are victims of Sunk Cost Fallacy. When AOL was purchased by Time Warner, it seemed to be a media match made in heaven. But a year later it became apparent the two cultures could not combine. Time Warner CEO, Gerry Levin, displayed total faith in the new megamedia company and promised it would work out in the end. Well, it didn't. This Sunk Cost merger mistake ended up soaking Time Warner billions of dollars.

One symptom of Sunk Cost fallacy is your tendency to invest more based on what you have already spent. Another symptom is to keep working on a project that has little chance of success, even if you put more time into it. I really like the notion of never quitting—ever. But that relates more to your passion than something you continue because of the money already invested.

Would you like to avoid Sunk Cost fallacy in the future? Then look at any investment you currently have and make a decision now on whether you would buy it again. If your answer is no, sell it. If the answer is yes, then you should buy more of it. One of my coaching clients spoke to a prospective client about liquidating some bad investments and buying a safe annuity instead. The client told the financial advisor he wanted to keep the investment until it regained its value. Well, the likelihood of the investment decreasing is greater than its chances to increase. It is a much better decision to unload the investment now, unless you are willing to buy more of it.

One client bought Yahoo at $426 per share and saw it decrease to $26 because he didn't want to ink his losses. When asked why he did nothing as it tanked, he said, "I didn't want to sell and take a loss."

As long as he didn't cash it in, there was a chance it would regain value.

NINE
Judgment Heuristic

Do you sometimes make judgments without sufficient information? Do you just react? Amos Tversky and Daniel Kahneman, two psychologists widely regarded as the founders of behavioral economics, suggest that most people use Heuristics, or shortcuts, to make conclusions on incomplete and often limited information. These mental shortcuts have a great bearing on how people make decisions.

Daniel Kahneman observed that human judgment can be produced in two ways. One is a rapid, associative, automatic, and effortless intuitive process, and the other, a slower, rule

"Why make a decision when a reaction is quicker"

governed, deliberate, and effortful process. While the first approach often results in errors and mistakes, it is used more often than the more diligent second approach.

You probably use Judgment Heuristics every day.

One of my friends saw a US Congressman on TV and immediately said, "You know how to tell when a Congressman is lying, his lips are moving." This is an obvious stereotype, but a surprisingly common sentiment. We disregard computer spam messages, but read the same message when it comes from a friend.

You jump in a car and put your foot on the brake before you start the ignition without thinking. When you pull up to a yellow light, you press the gas pedal harder and speed through. These are all Judgment Heuristics. These are also the simplifications helping you avoid taking the time to make hundreds of daily decisions. Your investments go up, it's a good day.

They go down, it's bad. These shortcuts are also stereotypes to make sense of the world. Interest rates go down, stocks will likely go up. Inflation goes up, we should buy gold. While there is a lot more detail to consider, these are the Judgment Heuristic shortcuts helping you avoid confusion.

One of my coaching clients heard a prospective client complain about market volatility. He wanted to put them into an annuity but the client had a bias against annuities gained from a television special discussing poor sales practices. So the financial advisor instead renamed the annuity an "insured investment."

That made all the difference.

TEN

Extremeness Aversion

People with "Extremeness Aversion" are more likely to play it safe by staying in the middle. The middle option is usually the most desirable.

In one study, two Minolta cameras were offered costing $169 and $239. The sales volume between the two was evenly split. But another camera was offered at $469. The medium priced camera of $239 was now preferred over the cheaper model 2:1.

I tell my coaching clients to present three options.

The middle one will usually be selected. Recently during a speech, an attendee approached me with three cards. He told me to select one. When I picked the middle, he turned the card over, "You picked right."

> *"When evaluating two choices, I always go for the middle"*

Come to think of it, I never looked at the other two cards. They probably had the same line. Last week, a meeting planner asked what topics I speak on. I mentioned, "How to Read Your Client's Mind," "Peak Performance," and "Behavioral Investing." She picked the middle topic on "Peak Performance."

Extremeness Aversion can cause you to make some very mediocre decisions in your portfolio. You may avoid risk you should take and accept risk you should avoid. Staying in the middle will prevent you from recognizing when the market is overbought or undervalued.

This is the magic of contrarian investing.

Contrarians go against the herd and take more risk than the rest, making millions in the process. They also have the courage to sometimes take a limited, yet measured extreme position.

I spoke many years ago to the California Funeral Directors Association. I asked one attendee how he was emotionally able to sell coffins to bereaved families.

Coffins range from $500–$70,000. He rarely sells the $70,000 coffins and yet almost always never sells the $500 models either. It is very common for family members to skip over the cheapest coffins before settling on a more expensive one. Obviously the higher price, the more profit. So when you see a TV ad for "as low as" you know those are simply loss leaders few ever buy.

Extremeness Aversion may also prevent you from making big money. Wouldn't you have loved to invest $1,000 into Google when it was a start up? Wouldn't you have adored buying Apple when it first introduced the I-Phone? Conversely, would it have been nice to have the foresight to have sold Enron and Lehman Bros. a year before they went bankrupt?

While it's unlikely you will catch the knife edge of perfect timing, Extremeness Aversion prevents you from taking this kind of risk and will also cause your returns to be consistently ordinary.

Depending on your age, a way to overcome Extremeness Aversion is to take 10% to 20% of your portfolio and invest with more risk. You should also use the rule of 100: 100 minus your age indicates the amount you could invest with more risk, like equities, high yield bonds, IPO's and alternative investments. Your age would be the safe money portion to invest in products like annuities, CDs, and investment grade bonds.

ELEVEN
Prospect Theory

Prospect Theory was created by Amos Tversky and Daniel Kahneman to explain how people make uncertain choices. It has three important features:

1. Changes to wealth are experienced more emotionally than changes to levels of wealth.
2. We feel more emotion in the pain of loss than the joy of gain.
3. We experience loss independently rather than in relationship to the total value of our investments.

Bill told his financial adviser he objected to putting any money in emerging markets because they were too risky and unpredictable. He also didn't want any exposure to derivatives, which Warren Buffett once called, "Financial weapons of mass destruction." His portfolio was worth $10 million. He was moderately aggressive in his risk tolerance with 15 years before retirement.

He also had no income needs. But Bill viewed the risk in his portfolio in isolation. Any loss bothered him. While an investment in emerging markets and derivatives on their own can be extremely volatile, using those investments to balance a portfolio is a good means to allocate and manage risk while gaining larger returns. Counter-intuitively, riskier investments in proportion can actually help minimize overall risk. There can be more risk by investing too heavily in one asset class no matter how safe it seems.

Creating a portfolio is like building a house from the foundation up. Starting in the basement with US treasuries, the first floor might represent stocks while the second floor would include domestic equities. The attic could include the most aggressive investments such as emerging markets and derivatives. Yet having all US stocks would create more risk causing your portfolio to move in the same direction as the market. This is called correlation and may create more risk. Someone with Prospect Theory symptoms would view any risk on its own without relationship to the other asset classes and investments in the portfolio. If the attic has termites, the Prospect Theory homeowner would be tempted to sell the house without regard to the structural stability of the lower floors.

"Spending a dollar to save a dime"

Another example of Prospect Theory is spending a dollar to save a dime. Years ago my daughter Catherine lost her mobile phone. I told her to replace it with her own money. Catherine did a Google search and found the cheapest phone available. But then she made me drive to three Verizon stores as she tried to save $50.

After three hours, she found the phone. At the end of the day, it hit me. I spent nearly three hours of my time trying to save my daughter $50. So she was able to save some money, but it ended up costing me hundreds in lost time. I should have just taken her to the first store and paid the difference.

This next example hits even closer to home. One of my coaching clients decided to hire an assistant. He narrowed the field to the final five.

One candidate wanted $25 an hour while the others required between $18 and $20 an hour. He didn't want to overpay, yet his income was about $300,000 a year. This meant every hour he was on the telephone with a prospect or a client, he made $600. I asked him how many more hours he could be on the phone if he had an effective assistant; he said "lots." I then asked if the new assistant could save him one hour, would it really make any difference if he paid $25 or $18. He quickly admitted his mistake and hired the most qualified applicant without regard for the slight increase in expense.

This may seem like small potatoes. But I consulted with a billion dollar health care company many years ago. We were searching for a Senior VP and thought one candidate, while the most expensive, would be a better selection. The president of the company decided to pick a cheaper candidate rationalizing he didn't want his own bonus decreased. This is probably the worst example of Prospect Theory I have ever seen.

But our decisions are not so different. We look at expenditures in isolation without regard to how they impact other areas. We refuse to buy a new software program because it's expensive, not considering the time it will save. We buy a used cheaper car without regard to the repair expense it will incur.

Prospect Theory also causes us to make bad decisions in our pursuit of "free." For example, you go into a sports store hoping to buy a pair of socks. The socks you want have padded heels and toes while a cheaper offer tempts you with a less expensive two-for-one deal without the extra padding. Ten minutes later, you leave the store with three pairs of discounted socks. Well, you got a great deal unless you consider these are actually not the socks you wanted in the first place. This is called the "Zero Price Effect." Years ago I walked into a DVD store advertising a "Going out of business" sale. DVDs usually were $19, but these were discounted to only $5 each. I bought ten $5 DVDs. But when I watched the videos on my next airline flight, I realized why they were discounted.

None of the movies were worth watching. I went in the store originally to buy only one video for $19 and walked out with ten worthless ones for $50.

Many years ago Amazon started offering shipping for $1 on any purchase over $10. It was an instant success. But it wasn't until they started offering free shipping for all orders that sales really jumped. The free shipping offer dramatically increased sales to a level far exceeding the cost Amazon incurred for shipping.

"Isn't it amazing how much money people will spend to get something for FREE"

Could free shipping be considered found money?

If so, would you spend more due to free shipping? Remember "Marginal Propensity to Consume?"

Many of my fellow consultants and speakers don't yet get the concept of "free."

Often they charge $9 for shipping in addition to ever increasing sales tax. Many professional speakers don't realize by offering "no tax and free shipping" sales will increase even if prices commensurately increase to accommodate those expenses. I'm giving away my trade secrets as a speaker, but I'm sure you can use the same ideas in your business. Free is lost on the airlines.

When each airline competes in the same market, prices are driven down. But once you are on board, instead of "free," they charge for every extra fee they can get charging $15 for a sandwich and $5 for a pillow.

"Airlines are getting so cheap they are now charging for emotional baggage"

One comedian said airlines are getting so cheap they are now charging for "emotional baggage." Most businesses are not quite that cutthroat.

TWELVE
Arbitrary Coherence

A re you influenced by the low discount prices advertised in the newspaper? Are you persuaded to spend more because the price is discounted from the MSRP sticker price? You could be a victim of "Arbitrary Coherence."

You probably know how much a carton of milk costs. How much would you pay for a beer or a loaf of bread? The amount you are willing to pay for a gallon of milk is influenced by your past expenditures. These past purchases create anchors to all future purchases. In one study by Duke University professor Daniel Ariely, students were asked to write down their social security number. They then bid on an expensive bottle of wine. It was a medium bodied, medium intensity; nicely balanced red, rated a lofty 86 points from "Wine Spectator" magazine.

"I don't know how much it costs, I still want a discount"

The second bottle of wine, a 1996 Hermitage Jaboulet LaChapelle, the finest since 1990, had a 92 rating from "Wine Advocate" magazine. The students were also shown four other products to bid on. A cordless keyboard, a mouse, a graphic design book, and a one pound box of Belgian chocolates. The students were then asked to write down the last two digits of their social security number at the top of the page.

Lastly, they were told to write those numbers again next to each of the items there were bidding on in the form of a price. For example if the last two digits of a social security number were 33, the price was written as $33. Lastly they were asked to indicate with a simple yes or no whether they would be willing to pay that amount for each of the products. When the students finished answering, they were asked to write down the maximum amount they would bid for each product.

The students making the highest bids would be announced and pay for the products. They were asked if writing down their social in any way influenced the final bids. All of them denied it. But when the bids were analyzed, the students with the highest ending social security numbers, from 80 to 99, bid the highest for the products. While those with the lowest ending social security numbers, from 1 to 20, bid the lowest.

The top 20%, on average, bid $56 for the cordless keyboard, while the bottom 20% bid only $16. In the end, the students with the social security numbers ending in the highest 20% bid 216% to 346% more than the students with the lowest social security numbers.

The study has one more interesting aspect. While the willingness to pay for each of these items was arbitrary based on the social security number, it was also coherence to the product's perceived value relative to the other. While the students were willing to pay a certain price for one product, for example the 1998 wine, they were willing to pay even more for the 1996 wine.

So Arbitrary Coherence linked to an anchor, like MSRP, naturally caused the students to pay more.

If you go to Target to buy a coffee maker with an MSRP of $20, but then see another at $40 with more features, you would naturally assume that the more expensive coffee maker is twice as good as the cheaper model. It's almost like a peg in the ground anchoring all your future decisions.

Years ago I saw a Porsche 911S on a lot in Los Angeles.

It wasn't the color I wanted, so I told the salesperson to order a blue model with a black top. The price was nearly $110,000. After six months, I got tired of waiting and saw nearly the same car in Pasadena. This one had the same features as the one I ordered for $98,000, but with a gray top. As I negotiated, I remember thinking anything below $110,000 will be a good deal. So the first expensive car anchored me for all future Porsche purchases.

Whether or not it was worth $98,000 was irrelevant.

It was cheaper than the $110,000 model I had on order.

One of my friends vacationed in Acapulco recently and bragged about the massage he got for $35. He was a real fan of massages, but couldn't bring himself to spend $60 back home in Orange County. He was anchored in his massage price expectations and influenced by Arbitrary Coherence in relationship to that cheap price.

THIRTEEN
Anchoring

As I mentioned in the section on arbitrary coherence, "Anchoring" occurs in many areas of your life. You went on an Italian vacation last year and are now dissatisfied with a trip to a California beach.

I went helicopter skiing many years ago in British Columbia, Canada. We spent a week flying to the most beautiful, picturesque slopes in North America. The conditions were perfect with powder up to our knees. I didn't ski in resort areas for the whole next year having been

> *"That's not the deal I got last time"*

spoiled from the amazing heli-ski experience. You might call it being anchored in that skiing in a normal resort was no longer good enough. When I was young, a cup of coffee was only a dollar. Now, as I travel around the world, I can tell the value of a local currency by paying attention to what coffee shops charge.

Even now when I pass Starbucks, I can't bring myself to pay $5 for even the largest cup of latte.

Can you remember the last time you went to a garage sale? You found a tray that would have cost $200 in a consignment store. Yet at the garage sale it was only $49. But every other item at that Saturday morning sale was no more than $10. You were anchored. There is no way you would've paid $49 for a silver tray when every price you saw was less than $10. The lyrics of a popular song state, "Many know the price of everything and the value of nothing." Anchoring may influence your price/value decision so much that you forget value and depend too much on price.

> *"Many know the price of everything and the value of nothing"*

FOURTEEN
Recency Bias

What you heard most recently may have the most impact on your future decisions. People tend to overweigh recent events considering the probability of outcomes. If someone just lost money in the market, they will be shy at the prospect of losing money again. But if the market runs in five year cycles, investors will be surprised at the next downturn. They often don't effectively plan since the recent memory of an increase causes them to expect more of the same.

"What I heard yesterday is the truth"

This is what happened in the real estate bubble ending in 2008. Ten years of rising property values simply creates even higher expectations.

One of my realtor friends has a bumper sticker that says, "Lord please help me save the money I make in the next boom cycle." But of course he won't. Because every time there's a boom in business, he will expect it to last forever. Recency Bias indicates a tendency to believe things we just hear has even more impact than our own common sense. If a friend tells me he just bought a condo in a distressed area and believes it will go up in price by 20% in the next six months, I'm influenced to think I should put money in real estate also.

> *"Lord please help me save the money I make in the next boom cycle"*

But more to the point, if you notice a mutual fund that increased last week, you will also be influenced to pour money in thinking it will keep increasing in value. Many analysts believe you should never invest in a stock that recently improved. Instead, they try to find undervalued, not yet noticed stocks, ripe for a move in the near future. By the time you hear about a stock, it is usually too late to buy.

One of my clients sells annuities. His best year was 2008. The stock market decreased dramatically and everybody could see its fall. But instead of investing in the market at a low value, he was able to convince seminar attendees to transfer their money out of the stock market into safe annuities. This is a great strategy for seniors who really can't deal with volatility. But probably not such a great idea for those under 50 influenced by what they heard last week assuming the same will happen for the foreseeable future.

FIFTEEN
Overweight Memorable Events

People tend to overweight information that comes most easily to mind. The more vivid (extreme) memories are the best remembered.

For example, "The market crashed 8% yesterday; therefore it is likely to crash tomorrow." "Overweighting Memorable Events" may seem a lot like Recency Bias except it lasts longer. In 1987, the stock market dropped 15% in one day. It seemed like the end of the world if you had money at risk. Many sold their stock

"What I remember best is the most believable"

positions and went to cash. On 9/11, terrorists crashed airliners into the World Trade Center buildings. That memorable event caused many investors to completely avoid airline stocks. It also caused flyers to avoid airline travel for a couple of years.

I was on a flight to New York City recently sitting next to a white knuckle flyer. He was so scared, he was hyper-ventilating. I tried to calm him down saying how safe flying was. The truth is he's more likely to die from electrocution in a bathtub than crashing in a commercial jet. That didn't seem to help his mood. All he talked about were the planes hijacked on 9/11.

Another example of overweighting memorable events is called "Snakebite Bias." You lost money in real estate last year so you will never invest in it again.

The oil and gas market turned against you a few years ago, so you'll never consider putting money there in the future. You bought a Mercedes years ago and it turned out to be a lemon. So you tell your wife you'll never buy another.

An NBC documentary, "To Catch a Predator," has been seen by millions of people. Another NBC documentary exposed annuity salespeople at their worst. In one episode, an unethical salesperson actually wore a white belt with matching patent leather shoes. He looked the part of a flim-flam insurance agent which is part of the reason the salesperson was highlighted in the program. He told the seventy year old prospect an annuity was not only a safe investment but would grow by 10% per year. There was no way he could truthfully make that claim. The host then appeared in the living room with a camera crew confronting the salesperson in the obvious lie. Anybody watching that program would be biased against ever buying an annuity. Yet an annuity can be a great investment for the right portfolio.

Overweighting Memorable Events like a TV program can cause you to be biased against a potentially good investment.

California where I live has a reputation for severe earthquakes. But major damage rarely occurs, save in some very vulnerable areas.

One example is Northridge, California home of the world's pornography industry.

Fifty percent of that industry was wiped out during the earthquake of the same name. Perhaps it was God's divine judgment? My house is about 75 miles south of Northridge and sustained a couple of stucco cracks.

The San Francisco earthquake occurred a few years earlier and was even more severe. In fact, I can still remember video of a freeway overpass collapsing. Yet I still don't have earthquake insurance. It would be an extra $1,000 per year premium with a $1,000 deductible. I've lived in California for 43 years and never had damage more severe than what a paintbrush and a quart of stucco could fix. Yet the Northridge and San Francisco earthquakes created memorable advertising events that made a lot of money for earthquake insurance companies.

SIXTEEN
Deadline Bias

The longer you defer a decision, the less likely you are to make one. Procrastination is a bigger enemy to your financial survival and independence than even bad advice.

I often tell my friends bad breath is better than no breath of all. Making a bad investment decision is better than making no decision at all. You need to give yourself deadlines for decisions. Of course this is easier said than done since most of us would rather stay with the status quo. Many also deal with indecision by avoidance. Many of my coaching clients mention their own investment clients procrastinate to the point of self-sabotage. Nearly every week I hear about a client who won't get documents back to implement a financial plan; even though they agreed it was the right thing to do. Another example is a client who procrastinates booking a second appointment. Perhaps making a decision to move money is as painful as going to

> *"I think I will put that off until never"*

the dentist knowingly without anesthetic. Of course when the worst happens and losses occur, they blame the market or the economy instead of themselves.

Two behavioral economics researchers, Tversky and Safir, gave students $25 to complete a survey. Some were given five days, some 21 and some no deadline at all. 66% of the five day people turned it in. 40% of the 21 day people turned it in and only 25% of the no deadline people turned in the survey. The more time you have to do a task, the more likely it is that you won't do it at all.

"Bad breath is better than no breath at all"

The remedy is to assign a deadline for every important task. If you keep a "to do" list, associate a deadline with it. It doesn't matter when, but you have a date to get it done. If you are unwilling or don't have the time to assign a date for completion, accept that you will never do it.

SEVENTEEN
Overconfidence Bias

Your guess may seem more reliable than even the advice of experts. "Overconfidence Bias" may cause you to believe too much in your own ability and the accuracy of your predictions. When asked to estimate a range of possibilities with 95% certainty, people guessed wrong 40% of the time. For example, if I asked you to estimate within a 95% range what price an investment would be within a year, you'd be wrong 40% of the time.

Let's try it. What is the size of the Sahara Desert?

All you have to do is answer with a range and be 95% (not 100%) confident. Five inches to 1 billion miles would be 100% confident. But no guesses are 100% confident. So what is your range in square miles for the Sahara?

The answer is 3.5 million square miles. Were you close? Did your range include this number? No participant in any of my seminars so far has answered correctly.

One aspect of overconfidence bias is how much time you give yourself to do a task. Are you always running against a deadline? Are you late for appointments?

Do you set expectations sometimes too high to deliver?

This is one of my biggest problems. I set my expectations very high for projects and often give myself too little time to do it. One of my tennis friends hits the ball too hard for his ability. He makes a lot of mistakes and loses to players he should beat. I sometimes tease him with a quote from the movie "Top Gun," "Your ego is writing checks your body can't cash." Another friend is constantly late. She admitted rarely allotting quite enough time. This is another example of overconfidence bias. Your ego tells you to leave 20 minutes early for a trip that really takes 30.

> *"Your ego is writing checks your ability can't cash"*

When someone tries to sell their home without the help of a real estate professional, it's called a FSBO, or For-Sale-By-Owner. This describes 20% of the homeowners each year who try to save 6% commission. But they nearly always underestimate the complexity of the job and overestimate their sales ability. In fact, the United Homeowners Association, a non-profit group, stated a majority of all FSBO's each year end up being sold by traditional brokers. It's true that a FSBO can save 6%. Yet on average, the homeowner's overconfidence and lack of experience caused their home to be sold for a lower price than utilizing the services of an experienced broker. There are many reasons for this. Some FSBO sellers negotiate too low a price, while others overestimate the value of their home and fail to entertain more realistic offers. Sometimes they are "anchored" by what they paid for the house years earlier. But there's another reason. Buyers know when the house is being sold FSBO.

They also know the seller is saving 6% by not using a broker. So the offers are often lower than if the homeowner used a broker.

Sixty percent of investors don't use the services of a professional financial adviser. Yet on average they achieve 8% below the market indexes. The typical mutual fund manager who spends every day trying to uncover brilliant investments is very lucky if they meet the market average. In most years only 25% of these professional managers get better returns than the indexes.

To give you an example of how Overconfidence Bias creates poor returns, Brad Barber and Terrence O'Dean at the University of California, Davis, analyzed the performance of individual investors from February 1991 through December 1996. During that five-year period, the average return was 17.7%, slightly less than the benchmark indexes. But surprisingly, they discovered 20% of households trading more than 10% of their portfolio each month, earned an average return of only 10%. There's only one reason why frequent traders don't use a professional broker. Firstly, to save commissions, and secondly, overconfidence that their skills are superior to the professional. Do-It-Yourselfers consistently achieve lower returns without even considering the commissions they would pay to professionals.

If you overestimate your abilities, try hedging your investments. For example, use a stop loss or an option to make sure your stock doesn't drop below a pre-determined threshold. If you have Overconfidence Bias, hedge your bets. While difficult, you will save many sleepless nights.

Psychologists believe Overconfidence Bias sufferers possess three major problems:

1. They have an illusion of control. They believe they can influence uncontrollable events.

2. They believe successful outcomes are the result of their skill, while bad results are just bad luck.

3. They have hindsight bias. They convince them selves a prediction of past mistakes would have made them less vulnerable to futur e ones. For example if I lose money on an oil trade, I feel confident that the knowledge I gained will prevent losses in the future.

Harvard Psychologist Eileen Langer calls Overconfidence Bias, "Heads I win, tails it's chance." The notion here is when things work out to confirm your actions and beliefs; they are a testament to your ability.

But when things don't work out, the mistakes are attributed to factors beyond your control.

Another aspect of Overconfidence Bias is the conviction you should invest in what you know. This partially explains why employees of major corporations usually allocate more than 35% of their retirement accounts to the stock of the company they work for. Despite creating more risk, most financial pros believe no investor should put more than 10% of their retirement assets into the shares of their own company. When I play tennis and get to a tiebreaker, I often try to hit the biggest serve I can muster. This is due to the mistaken belief that my game is as good as I think it is.

"Heads I win, tails its chance"

The right way to play a tiebreaker is to be conservative and get the balls in, hoping your opponent will make more mistakes that you.

Some symptoms of overconfidence bias are:

- You put too much money into one investment.
- You think you are beating the market, when you're not.
- You make frequent trades with a discount broker.
- You believe selling your own home without a broker is smart.
- You don't compare your investment rate of return against the indexes.
- You think investing what you know is better than being well diversified.

EIGHTEEN
American
Expressaphobia

It is not only likely you will spend more with a credit card, it is probable. America's average household debt is $18,000. As of 2005, the American family had an average of six credit cards.

Even though Americans have been deleveraging since 2007, the use of credit cards is actually going up. In his book, *Why Smart People Make Big Money Mistakes*, Gary Belsky called this "American Expressaphobia." This is kind of like the old line, "What do you mean I don't have money in my account, I still have checks." Many years ago MIT researchers Prelac and Simester conducted a real-life auction for Boston Celtics tickets during the Robert Parish, Larry Bird era. The participants in the auction were told to pay in cash if they were the high

> *"What do you mean I don't have money in my account, I still have checks"*

bidder. The other half were told they would have to pay with credit cards. The researchers then averaged the sealed bids and discovered credit card submissions were twice as much as the cash bidders.

It seems through Mental Accounting, a purchase with a credit card was somehow less expensive than a purchase using cash. Because of this, it is small wonder so many families are in high levels of debt, spending too much on plastic.

But this monetary devaluation is not just limited to credit cards. It went on steroids with home equity lines of credit. In 2003, I applied for a home equity line to construct a second story on my house. The equity line interest was about 4.5%. It was even tax deductable.

One weekend, my wife and I went to Home Depot to pick up some bathroom hardware. In the corner of my eye, I was attracted to a 56 inch big-flat screen TV. I told Merita not to worry; we would just pay for the big screen out of the home equity line. I called the salesperson over and in the middle of asking questions about the TV, realized what a dumb purchase it would be. In a rare lucid moment, I asked myself, "Would I pay for the TV pulling out $1000 in cash?" The cash would have been more vivid and painful coming out of my billfold. Brought back to my senses, I wasn't willing to pay with green and luckily passed it up.

I belong to the Palisades Tennis Club in Newport Beach, California. After a match my friends often have a beer. A few of my friends pay in cash while the rest of us just charge drinks to our club account. It's shocking to see how high the bar tab can be each month.

One of my friends said he wants to "feel" the cost especially when he's had a few too many. I like his approach.

It's a self-policing system of feeling the pain and making a decision whether the purchase is worth the cost every time he opens his wallet.

Many financial advisors suggest cutting up your credit cards. But today many purchases can only be made with credit cards. Almost all airline flights require a credit card to buy anything onboard, even a drink. So a debit card seems to be the answer, as long as it doesn't include an overdraft account. Overdraft charges are as bad as using a high interest credit card.

NINETEEN
Default
Decision Making

According to Richard Thaler of the University of Chicago, many feel too overwhelmed or lazy to make a decision and often make none. Sometimes they don't have enough information or just want to avoid making a mistake.

You could decrease taxes by reallocating assets if you were more proactive in your investment account.

Many can add ten more years to life by stopping smoking or losing weight. But we procrastinate. Either way, by not making a decision, we have actually made one by default.

One couple procrastinated putting their money into a safe life insurance investment that included a "Procrastinating a decision is actually making one" death benefit. The husband was motivated to buy but the wife was hesitant. She wanted to think about it. A week became a month and then three. Default decision making took hold. The act of procrastinating making a decision became a decision not to buy. She came home from the store while her husband slept on the couch. Making dinner, she walked over and noticed he wasn't breathing. He died while she was cooking. Distressed days later, she called her advisor. But there wasn't much he could do. The money in her account was all there was. No life insurance, no death benefit because they never made a decision to buy. By not making a decision, she made a default decision of no.

In 1985, many American families had a double digit savings rate. By 1994, the same savings rate dipped to 5%. By 2006, the savings rate had decreased to less than zero. After the great recession of 2008, personal savings rates increased slightly to 2%. But this low level of saving only indicated the amazingly high addiction Americans have to consumption. Nearly every family has two big cars, big screen TVs and often takes expensive vacations. According to a new study, baby boomers born after 1945 actually think airline travel is a fundamental need on par with medical services.

Europeans save an average of 15% while the Japanese savings rate is 25%. The Chinese savings rate is 50%. But the bottom line is not making a decision to save or invest is worse than making the wrong decision. It is a default decision not to save.

The organ donation rate in the US is about 15%.

The main source of organ donations is from auto fatalities.

This means only 15% of drivers in America marked the box on their license application indicating a willingness to donate their organs. In Holland, the rate is 85%. What could be the difference between the US and Dutch donation rates? The answer is surprisingly simple. Written on the US driver's license application is the question, "Mark the box if you are willing to donate your organs in case of fatality." The default is failing to mark the box meaning you are unwilling to donate your organs. In Holland, Sweden, and Finland, the question is worded a different way. Their application contains the sentence, "If you are unwilling to donate your organs, please mark the box." By not marking the box, you have given permission to use your organs. This is a good example of how countries use default decision making in gaining greater compliance.

Many of my coaching clients present safe investment choices to their clients. Often the response is, "We want to think about it." A few days of this stall often progresses into a month or three months or no decision at all. I try to tell my clients to use a very aggressive but effective technique called the "Upfront Close," "If we decide to put together a financial plan, I hope you will implement it. If we put together a plan you don't like, tell me that too because I really want to do what's best for you. But I'd rather you not say, give me a few days, or weeks or months, and I'll get back to you. Because that tells me you do not have enough information to make an informed decision. The truth is, you will not hurt my feelings by saying no, is that fair?"

It's a very effective technique to get people to make a decision, and actually the best thing for them. The worst thing a financial advisor can do is allow a client to procrastinate a decision to the point of never making one at all.

One way I use default decision making in my coaching practice is to first book an appointment and tell my clients to change it later if necessary. My eye doctor sends out cards with an appointment they suggest.

They will follow up by telephone three days after.

The voice mail reports, "If you can't make it, please call. Instead of, "Call us if you want an appointment."

A few years ago, I made an online purchase for some office equipment. I noticed the price was $20 more than I expected. I went back to the order, line by line, and couldn't figure out where the extra $20 came from. Finally, after ten minutes, I noticed one line that said, "If you do not want the one year maintenance contract for $20, please mark this box."

This is a good example of how default decision making is used to manipulate.

Some of my clients market their services using seminars and pre-book appointments for all the attendees.

They also mention if the attendee needs to change the appointment to please call. Since we are natural decision defaulters, these techniques require a more volitional decision to change.

TWENTY
Contrast Bias

When I bought my Porsche 911S Carrera, the salesperson explained the options I could pick from. There was the Bose sound system, the leather interior, the S performance package including a bigger engine, the 3mm spacers for the rear wheels, as well as many, many other options. I don't think there was an option I didn't take. The salesperson admitted later that buying a Porsche is basically paying for a chassis, seat and an engine while everything else is an option. I started wondering why I was so open to accepting the option suggestions. And then it hit me. The basic Porsche was only about $65,000. And every option cost from $1,000–$5,000, seemingly cheap by comparison to the base price.

> *"Only give me two choices. I don't want to think that hard"*

There are those who say every decision we make is influenced by contrast. We pick a restaurant based on the price relative to similar restaurants in the area. We select an airline flight based on the expense compared to other airlines flying to the same destination. We price a house not based on its value, instead relative to other properties that have sold in the last six months.

We invest in relative prices rather than value.

"Contrast Bias" also makes it very difficult to invest wisely. We resist putting money in stocks because they seem expensive compared to prices a week ago. We put our money at risk because interest-rates are lower than the last time we looked. When I don't play tennis for a few weeks, my game is usually so good it seems as though I never took a break. But then after a few days, my game goes downhill dramatically. The difference is with a few weeks off, there's nothing to compare it to.

But when I play four days in a row, I'm constantly comparing my game to the last time I played and become increasingly frustrated.

One example of how Contrast Bias influences you is "The Decoy Effect." A realtor in Phoenix, Arizona took a buyer to a million-dollar property. Unfortunately the house had no view, overgrown front yard, weeds, and brown spots in the backyard. Even the pool was desperately in need of cleaning. The interior of the house was structurally good, but it still needed paint and new carpet. During the showing, the realtor kept talking about what a great deal it was.

Later that day, the realtor then took the couple to another property offered at the same price of $1 million.

But this house had a beautiful view, perfect landscaping, gorgeous pool, and actually 500 more square feet added to the floor plan. The couple made their decision to buy in less than 30 minutes. One can say the second house was worth $1 million and the first house was not. But by showing the fixer-upper initially followed by the beautiful dollhouse, a contrast was created that was too tempting for the buyers to pass up.

Duke University behavioral economist, Daniel Ariely noticed a premier business magazine, "The Economist," used the decoy effect to brilliantly sell subscriptions. At first they offered a choice between the "Internet only" subscription at $59 and the "Print/Internet" subscription for $125. Later they changed the offer using the Decoy Effect and increased subscription sales dramatically. Ariely decided to test it with his own students. 68 of them selected the Internet only subscription, while 32 students chose the print/Internet combination for $125. Ariely then introduced the choice of a print only subscription for $125, the same price as the $125 print/Internet subscription. Now with three choices, only 16 selected the Internet only subscription. Nobody chose the print only subscription for $125, while 84 students picked the print/Internet subscription for $125.

Having a decoy introduced in the middle of the two choices dramatically impacted the value buyers perceived in each "Economist" magazine subscription offer.

In a University of Arizona study, students part of a social psychology experiment were told to rate the next person they met based solely on attractiveness. Being rated by students as to how good you look may seem superficial. But this is how experimental psychologists do research. In another part of the study, students in a waiting room were shown pictures of models of the opposite sex and asked to rate the beauty of the living, breathing person they met later. The contrast between the model pictures and the real-life person was dramatic.

The normal people were consistently rated less attractive as a result of the participant seeing the model photos first. When the

"Take a friend who is a little less attractive to a bar or party. This will cause you, by contrast, to look even better"

photos were not presented, the normal looking, real life people were rated as much more attractive. The notion here is that if you're going to meet somebody at a bar or a party, take a friend who is a little less attractive. This will cause you, by contrast, to look even better.

Contrast bias also applies to small purchases. It's very easy to see the difference between a $1,000,000 house and a $500,000 dwelling. Yet noticing the differences between small purchases like a gallon of milk for $4.59 and $4.65 over a year will have a much greater impact on your cash flow and net worth than larger purchases made infrequently.

We buy a new home every five to ten years and a new car every three to six years. But we buy milk, bread, gas and other small purchases almost every day. These purchases make up the bulk of what we spend. So paying more attention to your every day purchases remembering Contrast Bias will have a much bigger impact on your disposable income.

TWENTY-ONE
Hyperbolic Discounting

D o you remember the old Popeye animation? Wimpy used to say, "I will gladly pay you Tuesday for a hamburger today." This is a good example of "Hyperbolic Discounting."

This concept suggests what you have today is more valuable than a larger gain tomorrow.

People act irrationally by overtly discounting the future. A bird in the hand is worth two in the bush? If you treat your investments that way, you are a victim. We spend too much focused on the things we want now at the expense of the wiser purchases we could make in the future. This is one of the reasons for such high credit card debt. People want something right now regardless of whether they can afford it. According to economists,

> "I will gladly pay you Tuesday for a hamburger today"

there should be no economic difference between desires now and purchases later. But behavioral economists know emotions make us all irrational.

It's sort of like Homer's hero Odysseus. The goddess Circe told Odysseus his ship would pass by the island of the Sirens. The singing from the island would lure ships onto the rocks. So Circe advised Odysseus to prepare for the Sirens' temptation by ordering his crew members to plug their ears with wax so they could not hear the Siren songs. They were also to lash Odysseus (without earwax) to the mast ignoring his pleas. Odysseus knew he would be tempted by the Siren songs just as we are distracted from investing adequately for retirement. Unfortunately, there's no one to lash us to the retirement savings mast. We have to resist the temptation to spend money now for a better reward in the future.

One of the most glaring problems of Hyperbolic Discounting is failing to contribute to retirement matching funds. Only 32% of those eligible for 401(k) matching contributed, even when the employer matched them dollar for dollar. The mental thought here is the dollar I own right now is worth more than the two dollars I will receive in the future. You have seen kids behave this way. They spend their allowance within 24 hours of their first paycheck and then ask you to cover their gas and other expenses.

In one study by researchers Madrian and Shea, default decision-making strategy was used to prevent Hyperbolic Discounting. In other words, companies would withhold retirement funds up to 10% of a worker's salary unless the worker specifically told the company not to do it. The result was a 50% greater participation rate than if the worker were asked for permission.

In some ways, putting money into a CD, annuity, or bond prevents an investor from hyperbolic discounting.

By nature of the investment, the money is locked up for a few months or years. This makes the money inaccessible for at least a short period of time.

"Short term is better than long term"

TWENTY-TWO
Home Bias

Do you believe American stocks and bonds are safer and include better performance than international issues?

Do you feel more comfortable investing in areas you know instead of balancing your portfolio with investments less familiar? If you answered yes to these questions, you may be a victim of "Home Bias."

Obviously, your portfolio needs to be properly balanced.

You need to have a well diversified portfolio with non-correlated assets. When one part of your portfolio tanks, the other should increase, making up for the loss. There are few exceptions to this, save the great 2008 recession. For nearly two years from 2007 to 2009, any asset class that could lose value did.

"I'll stick to my knitting"

Yet what you may seem more familiar with in your portfolio may not be the best investment. The US stock market, as measured by market capitalization or total money invested, only accounts for 44% of the total global equity market. According to John Nofsinger, in his book The Psychology of Investing, even the most sophisticated of investors believe that domestic stocks will have a higher return and be safer than international ones. This is home bias. From 2008 until 2010, both Canada and Australian stock markets outperformed the US indexes. For most of 2009–2010, the Euro increased against the US dollar. The emerging markets of Brazil, China, India, and even Japan outperformed US indexes. The Chinese GDP in 2010 increased by 8% while the US GDP increased only 2.2%.

Another example of home bias is to invest in what you know. If you owned real estate for 20 years, you are likely to continue to be attracted to this asset class.

My wife Merita loves gold. Nearly every conversation we have about investing includes her fondness of gold.

One of my clients ten years ago was based in Korea Town in Los Angeles. He speaks Korean and focused his practice toward that community. I remember Jim telling me how difficult it was to get his clients to diversify past real estate. He couldn't even bring them to consider life insurance.

On the one hand, home bias allows us to feel more confident, but allowing this bias creates more risk and decreases safety. Often investors mention their attraction toward bank CDs. Until recently, CDs paid less than 2% interest based on a six month term. Yet after inflation and taxes, they can actually lose money. But investors will rationalize the benefits of CDs because they are familiar.

TWENTY-THREE
How Men and Women Talk About Money

It was a strange appointment. Jill had been a financial advisor for many years and seen it all. She has male clients sure, but she usually got along better with the women.

They seemed more receptive. Even though she earned an advanced degree in finance, nothing seemed to impress her male prospects. Jill always had long, interesting and enjoyable conversations with women, but by contrast, short focused ones with men. Her satisfaction rate with women was always high. But doing business with men

> *"If you can't listen, how can you expect me to take your advice"*

seemed to frustrate her. They often acted like they knew more than she, which usually was incorrect. To boot, they would sometimes even defend their faulted opinions.

Women investors are different. They seem more willing to acquiesce to expertise. If men try to show how much they know, women are more deferential.

Women are willing to listen and ask questions even though they are just as informed as men. Women want to chat a little while they get to know someone, while men often want to get to the point quickly. Jill couldn't help wondering if she should limit her practice only to women instead of selling to both genders.

> "If momma's not happy, nobody's happy"

Are there communication differences between you and your spouse? Do you wish you could decrease your financial disagreements? Researchers have concluded your domestic happiness is in direct relationship to how well you communicate with your spouse about money. "If momma's not happy, nobody is happy."

Studies now suggest that 70% of financial decisions are currently influenced by women, while 58% of retail financial product decisions are directly made by them.

In the next three years, because of changing demographics, those numbers will only increase. The problem is that men are generally confused about the communication differences between men and women.

They may feel ill-prepared to talk about money in a meaningful way with their spouse. In most studies, the primary reasons for family conflict are money, sex, and children, in that order. Having raised three daughters, I would rather try to learn to communicate better with my wife than even my kids. I think my wife is more rational.

The Dilemma

Would you like to learn how to communicate with your spouse about money?

The answer lies in first, how much you know about the other.

Money for a man is about control, leverage and power. Money for a woman is often about safety and security. Women are concerned about security not only for herself, but mainly her kids. And that applies to grandkids as well.

A woman spoke to a friend about a co-worker she was having problems with.

The worker was a longtime employee and had a lot of friends in the company.

The woman's friend commiserated by relating it to a similar situation she had a couple of years earlier. The two talked for a few hours about how frustrating office politics were. Both felt like they had connected and greatly enjoyed being together. But when the woman related the same office story to her husband, he abruptly said, "Why don't you just fire the employee?," and then walked away. The two female friends spent a long period of time talking without offering solutions. In a sense, the purpose of the female to female conversation was not to reach a solution, but instead to connect. A quick remedy would have only shortened the conversation and diminished rapport and intimacy. But her husband offered a quick-fix which illustrated how he solved problems. It was also a comment supporting his sense of status. "How good could the advice have been?," she thought, "If it was given so quickly." Women often say they receive unsolicited and unwelcome advice from men. When a quick fix is suggested too early, the woman may feel diminished.

Men seem to possess a need to give advice. Recently, I rode in an elevator with a client before a presentation.

We were both discussing male/female communication patterns. One of my client's friends in the elevator overheard part of the conversation and offered to give both of us a lesson on how to treat women based on his 20 years of marriage. We immediately laughed because he just proved my point. Men tend to give unsolicited advice in an effort to communicate power and status in a conversation.

> *"Women communicate in an effort to gain intimacy and rapport. Men communicate to gain status and power"*

In communicating about money with women, try to avoid solving their concerns. First try to empathize.

Tell them about similar situations you've experienced.

Talk about how you felt when it happened. Discuss the emotions of other people involved. Women tend to think of success as defined by the number of intimate and lasting relationships they possess. Men often value themselves by taking inventory of their status and accomplishments, often measured by money. Linguist Deborah Tannen discusses this constant one-upmanship as "alignment." Men often try to position themselves higher than the person they're talking to, hence the bragging and verbal displays of ego. Almost like "My dad can take your dad."

In talking to men about money, allow them to position themselves above you. Your own level of self-confidence will dictate how high you will allow a man to align. But, by doing this, you will also give him a sense of security by granting more status in the relationship.

You might do this by saying, "I'm sure you know that," or, "As informed as you are, you have probably heard that. . . ." In a man's world, one gains status by superior knowledge and an ability to get others to follow. In a woman's world, status isn't the objective at all. Making intimate and supportive relationships is primary.

Women often complain about a male insensitivity.

Men sometimes complain about women "looping" or how long it takes them to get to the point. Women complain about a man's desire to shorten an otherwise enjoyable conversation by too quickly offering a solution or answer to a question.

Women often appreciate help and advice such as straightening out a decorating problem. But when it comes to an emotional concern about money, listen but don't solve until they ask for advice. The problem is, behind every tangible problem are emotional undercurrents.

I learned this recently when a female client mentioned her frustration. She planned out her company's annual convention, but her boss didn't even seem to notice. With every suggestion I gave to resolve her concerns, she went on to another problem. I finally realized that my focus toward solving her problems was only a hindrance to the flow of our conversation.

Sociologist Erving Goffman took this idea of alignment a step further. Men, when confronted with a problem, tend to elevate their status by trivializing or ignoring it, saying something like, "no big deal" and moving on in the conversation. But in discussing emotions with men, relate the problem to someone else's dilemma or mention it as a challenge you would like solved.

I heard a story recently of a female financial advisor who was trying to sell disability insurance to a male business owner. She mentioned the incidence of morbidity is much higher than mortality while illustrating the concept with a story. A surgeon who injured his hand was so distressed; he tried unsuccessfully to commit suicide because he was unable to provide for his family. She could have directly asked her client how he would feel unable to provide for his family without the story. But the client may have trivialized the emotion claiming he never worried about something so remote.

By hearing about someone else with that problem, he was able to preserve his own alignment to the advisor and accept the example without admitting he might be vulnerable.

What Women Want

Three things women buy are not related to discounts and blue light specials.

Women purchase:

1. Safety for their kids
2. Protection against disaster
3. Long term relationships.

In communicating with your partner, you need to stress the safety aspects and the impact it will have on her kids. In one study on annuities, 74% of a major insurance company's annuity sales were to women.

They are naturally more risk averse and focus on safety.

Annuities are able to provide a sense of safety a woman often craves.

Also, when you talk to women about their investments, mention you will be there in thick and thin.

You will be there for her. She wants to have a long term relationship. Men will tell three people how happy they are with a financial advisor. Women will tell 15. If you are a financial advisor, you will gain more referrals from one woman than ten men in your practice once you learn how to communicate with them.

Women generally don't like to talk to men about money because men diminish financial issues and often don't sound like they are listening. They also don't look like they are listening. When women listen, they make listening sounds and listening movements.

They make one word comments as they listen and constantly make facial expressions in reaction to what they hear.

Men will usually say nothing, look blank and sometimes disinterested. They may even look past you. Men can connect better with women about money if they can appear more attentive and supportive of what she is saying. At least nodding of the head as she talks. My wife told me a 30 minute story about one of our kids and I nearly fell asleep. I listened to her tell the same story to her sister and they spent two hours talking about it. Afterward, my wife accused me of not caring enough about our kids, otherwise I would have listened better. She was right and wrong. I care a lot about my kids but can't stay focused on the point as long as she can.

Three things women dislike most when talking to men are:

1. Men give women advice when they never asked for it in the first place.
2. Men interrupt women while they are talking.
3. Even though they look like they are, men often don't listen.

If you want a woman to listen to you, first treat her like the only person on Earth. That means you need to be totally attentive when she talks and interested in every emotion she communicates. If you can sincerely do this, you will find your "money miscommunication" will dissipate rapidly.

A few weeks ago, a female seminar attendee told me that she was at a car dealership. The salesman first asked where her husband was. She forgave his mistake and asked to look at the engine of a BMW she had an eye on. He opened the hood and proceeded to tell her where the engine block was and the cooling system, like he was talking to a third grader. She turned on her heel, went down the street and bought a new $100,000 750Li from the dealership down the street. Not being able to sell to women is also costing companies' money.

Communicating with the opposite sex is difficult, at best. Girls don't grow up communicating directly to the point with boys and boys don't share intimacies with girls. They play and talk generally in same sex groups. So chances are you have very little experience and insight into what the opposite sex is really thinking.

The problem is that if you don't know, you'll lose control and create conflict and misunderstanding. Pay attention the next time you are in front of the opposite sex partner. If you use these techniques, your money conversations will go a lot smoother.

TWENTY-FOUR
Confirmation Bias

We have a tendency to look for information that confirms our viewpoints, rather than falsifies it. Cornell University marketing professor Ed Russo asked students to evaluate restaurants. He showed them photographs and menus and asked the students to rate the establishment from one to ten; one being low, ten being high. Some students liked the menu and gave it a nine while other students were less impressed with the food or ambience and gave it a three. But then the students were taken inside the restaurant. They saw less appealing aspects such as torn cushions, dirt on the floor, and the poor state of the restrooms. Russo then asked the students to rate the restaurant again. Even after seeing the restaurant, the ratings varied slightly from the initial scores by only 10%.

"I only want to listen to what I already believe"

This is an example of "Confirmation Bias." This is our tendency to look for, and be persuaded by, information we have already accepted. Companies depend on this bias to build their brand. Bose headphones sound so good that when an "in-ear" model is introduced, your assumption will be that the Bose excellence will be maintained.

A few years ago, I decided on a vacation to Belize with my family. We booked the airfare and hotel and couldn't wait to go. But a hurricane traveled through the Caribbean for three days before the trip. My wife wanted me to cancel, but I just argued that it would miss Belize. I looked at the trajectory of the storm and the wind patterns and convinced myself that my family and our vacation weren't in jeopardy. It wasn't until the hotel called and said they were closing their property for five days that I relented. It wasn't that I didn't know a hurricane was going through the area, but I only listened to the news reports predicting the hurricane would pass north of Belize instead of through it.

Dick Winick of Cornerstone Research in Boston noticed when consumers select the same car year after year, they pay more. Buick owners paid an average of $1,500 more per vehicle while Mercedes owners paid an average of $7,500 more. The reason for the high premium is that loyal owners tend to be less skeptical and less willing to negotiate than the new brand buyers more inclined to negotiate the right deal. You will always get a better deal if you are prepared to walk away. This car ownership Confirmation Bias is also supported by constantly improving technology. Cars don't break down as often and have longer warranties.

So you are less likely to be disappointed with your purchase, also supporting Confirmation Bias.

Many years ago I went to a BMW dealership looking to buy a new 650. There were some beautiful cars on the lot. My wife Merita asked if I had ever driven a Porsche. I was curious and was focused on the 2003 Turbo on the far side of a lot. It was so fast, it flew below radar. I owned four BMWs before that trip, but I was now intrigued with buying a Porsche 911 Carerra.

Finally when I found one in Pasadena, I negotiated a $15,000 discount, unheard of in most Porsche dealerships. The car had been on the lot for three months and I was totally willing to walk away unless I got the right price. So the next time you want to buy a car, don't be in love with a model or the make.

Also, be willing to buy a car from a different manufacturer if you want to save money.

Whether cars, food, or even vacation spots, once you have developed even small preferences, you will view new information that supports those biases. This is probably the reason I have never been able to get my daughters to listen to what I don't like about their boyfriends. They are sold on whatever lad they are attracted to and disregard information that is inconsistent.

One of my clients was in search of a new office assistant.

He received 20 responses from an online ad.

The applicant he liked best currently had a job and when she phoned, it was while she was at her previous employer's office. I asked my client if he was bothered that the candidate was using company time to apply for a new job. He actually said, "I'm sure she won't do that when she works for me." Confirmation Bias strikes again. Three months after, he terminated her because she was using office time to do personal business.

One of my favorite hiring slogans is, "When people show you who they are, you should believe them."

> "When people show you who they are, you should believe them"

One part of how Confirmation Bias causes you to make poor investment decisions is Anchoring. Anchoring, discussed earlier, is the tendency to incorporate an idea or fact and use it as a reference point for future decisions.

Most of us have no idea that we anchor. In one study reported by Gary Belsky in his book, Why Smart People Make Bad Money Mistakes, students are asked to guess when Genghis Khan ruled Central Asia and the year he died.

They were then asked if it was before or after 151 AD.

The students didn't know that the year 151 was the arbitrary sum of adding 123 of the last three digits of a New York City zip code. So take a second right now and guess the year Genghis Khan died. You probably guessed way too low. Genghis Khan actually died in 1227 AD. You likely guessed wrong because you were anchored to 151.

Researcher Ed Russo asked a group of 500 MBA students to add 400 to the last three digits of their phone number and write it down. They were then asked to guess the year Attila the Hun was defeated by the Romans. When the written number was between 400 and 599, the defeat was guessed at 629 AD. But when the number was between 1,200 and 1,399, the average guess was 988 AD.

This affects your investment behavior in a profound way. How much should you spend for your wife's wedding ring? Many believe the answer is two month's salary. The correct answer is no more than you can afford. But DeBeers diamonds has advertised for decades that the cost of a wedding ring should be equal to two month's salary. You have been anchored by a diamond company's commercials.

In a 1987 study by the University of Arizona's Gregory North-craft and Margaret Neale, Confirmation Bias even affected real estate appraisal values. Working with real estate agents in Tucson, Arizona, researchers took one random group of brokers and asked them to appraise a home. The agents were given a ten page packet including the $65,900 asking price. Their average appraisal was $67,811. Later on, Northcraft and Neale brought a second group of agents to the same house. They conducted the same tour and distributed the same packet of information. But in this case, the listing price was $83,900. The average appraisal then came in $7,000 more than the first group at $75,190. The only difference between the first and second groups was the advertised listing price.

After I got married in 1990, I gave a speech in Torquay, England. We arrived in London, rented a car, and spent the night in Sussex. Merita wanted to spend the afternoon antiquing. She found a beautiful grandfather clock. I thought it was way too expensive at $1,000, but she was convinced it was a find, and worth $3,000 in the US. Back home, a dealer appraised it at $500. My beautiful wife was the victim of Anchoring and Confirmation Bias. She was unwilling to listen to a conflicting viewpoint.

People often hear what they want to hear. They focus on information that confirms their beliefs and explains away any evidence and information that conflicts.

As a result, many decisions are based on information that is inaccurate, incomplete, and/or simply wrong. Before the presidential election of 2008, Jay Leno did one of his "man on the street" interviews in Harlem, New York. He asked residents what they thought of Barack Obama. If they were willing to vote for him, Leno would then ask what they thought of Obama's pro-life stance, and what did they think of Obama's choice of Sarah Palin for his running mate.

In nearly every case, respondents thought Obama was right in being pro-life and anti-abortion. They agreed that having a woman as his vice-presidential running mate was a terrific idea. Actually the opposite was true.

Obama is pro-choice and his running mate was not Sarah Palin, it was Joe Biden. But because of Confirmation Bias, statements were accepted if it supported Obama or disregarded if it conflicted.

While Overcoming Confirmation bias is always difficult, there are ways you can mitigate it. First, get the opinion of at least two other sources before you make up your mind. Of course this may be easier said than done since you will probably be biased quickly toward your favorite piece of advice. Next, do your research. If you only have a hammer, you treat the whole world like it's a nail. If you only have a little information, you will project your decision based on it. So look at good and bad information with equal "If you only have a hammer, you treat the whole world like it's a nail" weight. Just as you would evaluate travel reviews, do the same with investment reviews. Nearly every broker, including Schwab, Ameritrade, and Scottrade, will make recommendations based on your retirement horizon and risk tolerance. You may still make some mistakes, but at least now they will be more educated ones.

> *"If you only have a hammer, you treat the whole world like it's a nail"*

TWENTY-FIVE
Neuro-Economics

One branch of behavioral economics is "Neuro-Economics." Neuroscientists look inside the brain with scanning tools like MRI and PET imaging. They look for brain wave patterns in response to the most motivating

"Me, Myself and I"

stimuli. Much of this research images blood flow in the brain. But waves of blood flow are in response to activities like the euphoria of playing a slot machine or the stress of a stock market loss.

Neuro-Economic researchers have discovered two key subsystems of the human brain. One is the Limbic/Paralmbic system and the other is the Analytic system. The Limbic/Paralimbic system is sort of the intuitive and emotional part of our psyche. It has a lot to do with emotions and also interpersonal responses.

The father of modern-day Psychoanalysis, Sigmund Freud, called this system the "Unconscious Brain." We have very little control over the Limbic system. It functions rapidly and causes us to feel immediate stress and joy without much conscious thought.

The other is called the Analytic System. It is centered in the frontal and parietal cortexes. This system controls our conscious thought process and is involved in calculation and future thinking. For example, if someone taught you how to play a game, the Analytic System would show you how to use the rules to win.

It also helps you focus on goals like saving money, making good retirement choices, and even selecting the best value when shopping. The Limbic system tempts you to buy ice cream even though you're on a diet, or to spend too much money drinking with friends because you're having a good time.

In one experiment, research subjects' brains were imaged while offered a choice between present and future rewards. The choices were $20 now or $23 a month from now. Both Limbic and Analytic systems showed brain wave activity. But when the offer changed to future rewards only: $20 in two weeks or $23 in one month, the Limbic or emotional system pretty much dropped out. The Analytic system kicked in. This study showed the more the Analytic system is engaged, the more it will direct you to focus on future rewards. If the Limbic system in your brain is more active, you are likely to choose what makes you feel good right now.

When the Limbic system is activated, it releases dopamine into the brain. Dopamine is the brain's pleasure chemical and induces feelings of happiness, arousal, alertness, and the pursuit of goals with even more focus.

This powerful chemical is also released when people use drugs. Cocaine and Heroin also cause the brain to release Dopamine. This has such a strong affect on the human brain; drug addicts will engage in nearly any illicit activity to get more of it. Unfortunately when drugs are used to excess, it diminishes dopamine receptors in the brain. This causes greater quantities of Cocaine and Heroin needed to get the same high.

Then a drug overdose can occur. Addicts struggle so hard to get high; they become toxic and the overdose eventually kills the user. Normal brain release of Dopamine without drugs is unlikely to kill you, but it also causes you to seek immediate gratification. This Dopamine quest can also influence your investment decisions. The emotionally driven Limbic system can make you greedy, cause you to overtrade, invest on impulse, and/or lose sight of your long-term retirement objectives.

I remember years ago in college spending a weekend in Las Vegas. We played craps at Caesar's Palace as soon as we got there. I was a very small time gambler with only $50 to my name. But I was on a lucky streak and made $100 within 20 minutes. The other players around the table made thousands compared to my pennies. One of the players actually tipped me $50 because I made him so much money while rolling the dice. I proceeded then to gamble my whole winning stack of $200 on one single bet. As you might expect, I lost all the money in the next five minutes.

If my Analytic system was operating effectively, I would've stopped gambling when I was ahead, or been smart enough to avoid gambling at all. But since my Limbic system was running wild, I only responded to the euphoric high. I was sure I would win thousands.

Your goal is to try to get both Limbic and Analytic systems in balance. For example, if you have money in the stock market and it corrects 10% in one day, the Limbic system senses danger and releases adrenaline as well as other stress hormones into the bloodstream.

This gives rise to anxiety, fear and what psychologists call, "Fight or Flight" response to the perceived threat.

You will feel sweaty palms, increased heart rate, and shallow breathing as you experience the emotions of loss. The problem is that loss avoidance will cause your Limbic system to tempt you to sell of all your investments avoiding further losses. Most people sell their good investments way too soon and keep their bad investments way too long. The reason, from a neuroeconomic perspective is the Limbic system overshadowing your Analytic system.

Of course the Limbic system is of some benefit. If a friend calls and invites you over to watch a game, you wouldn't want to wait an hour evaluating the various options. If you heard your favorite song, you might swing your wife around the kitchen compliments of your Limbic system. Telling her you like the song and going back to a good book may be an indication your Analytic system is in control.

There is hope. By becoming more emotionally intelligent and understanding the two brain systems, you can prevent yourself and your Limbic system from overreacting to losses or greed. For example, if the market drops 5% today, you may feel like selling your investments.

Try to project ahead the next six months and imagine what a spontaneous sale may do to your portfolio. Conversely, if the market drops 5% today, try to remember the last correction you experienced and how long it took the market to recover.

Don't fall prey to your Limbic system. When it comes to investments, support your Analytic system.

The Limbic system helps you experience the immediate joy of life. But allowing it to control you and your investments is a little like a two-year-old screaming in a fit when prevented from playing with a favorite toy.

You probably know someone who has very poor emotional control. Try not to be one of them while investing.

TWENTY-SIX
Optimism Bias

People tend to be overconfident about their own abilities and the outcome of their plans. Nearly 90% think they are above average drivers, less likely to get into an accident than the regular Joe. This is so pervasive, there is a psychological term for those who accurately assess their own abilities: clinically depressed. This is one of the reasons why drivers text even though there is a high likelihood of an accident.

One corollary to overconfidence is "Optimism Bias." People tend to be very confident about their own abilities and the outcomes of their plans. We often stay optimistic because we only remember the good things that happen and forget the bad. Recently during a Highway Patrol video, subjects were given alcoholic beverages and asked to drive a controlled obstacle course. Before the drive they were asked to rate their own level of

"I am superman, leaping tall buildings with a single bound"

intoxication. All the subjects were having fun, but didn't admit to feeling impaired. They were also asked to rate their confidence in successfully navigating the course. After only two drinks, many of the drivers hit pylons on the course. Obviously in real life, pylons could have been cars or even pedestrians.

In a 1997 study by Columbia University finance professor Gur Huberman, research concluded people tend to invest most frequently in things they know. In the 1980s, the monopolistic AT&T was ordered to be broken up by a Federal US Anti-Trust court. Huberman looked up the stock ownership records of the resulting seven, "Baby Bells." He discovered in all but one state, Montana, people held more shares of their local AT&T remnant phone companies than any of the other baby bells. This may make sense if your local phone company was the best of the seven. But odds are 7–1 against your local company emerging as the best choice.

Another example of Optimism Bias, is the "invest in what you know" behavior of many investors in their retirement plans. Most employees invest at least a third of their retirement plan selection into their own company. Many financial advisors recommend no more than 10% of your retirement program allocation in your own company. Yet this is precisely what happened to Enron employees before its famous bankruptcy.

Many employees found their retirement plan worthless because they were overly optimistic that Enron stock would consistently increase. Optimism trumps even common sense.

TWENTY-SEVEN
Disposition Effect

Terrance O'Dean, researcher at the University of California, Davis, noted investors were more likely to sell stocks that had risen than sell losing stocks. Instead of keeping stocks that were likely to be stable, they sold them. Stocks that investors sold, outperformed stocks held onto by 3.4 percentage points. Investors can write a loss off their taxes (offset) yet they hold onto losing stocks when they should be selling them.

Many investors believe they can time the market.

Sell and buy at the perfect time, making money when everyone else is wondering what to do. Many think if they know an investment like the back of their hand, they will always make money. If you watch CNBC frequently, you get the sense commentators can give you inside information allowing you to trade with constant success. Nearly every

"Why do I always seem to buy high and sell low"

financial program features a host asking an expert guest what they own and what they should avoid as if they had a crystal ball.

This mistake of buying and selling at the wrong time is called the "Disposition Effect." Behavioral economists Meir Statman and Hersh Shefrin recognized this emotional tendency is caused more by pride and regret, than by logic and rationality. One client bought Google in its early stages and held it only for a year. Google, at the time, was a stock rising dramatically faster than the S&P index. The same client bought Yahoo at $400 per share and watched it decrease to $26 per share. Apparently the client didn't know which to sell and keep.

In one study conducted by Terrance O'Dean, researchers evaluated tens of thousands of individual investors at one large discount investment brokerage firm. They concluded individual investors usually sold winning stocks too early and held losers too long. In a study of 60,000 households, O'Dean and Barber evaluated stock investor performance during one five-year period in the 1990s. They discovered the average household earned an average return of 17.7%, close to the 17.1% return of the benchmark index. But surprisingly, the 20% of households who traded the most turned over 10% of their portfolio each month and earned an average return of only 10%.

Compare this to a typical mutual fund manager.

This is somebody who probably has an MBA and spent a lifetime working in the pursuit of discovering brilliant investments ideas. Yet the same expert will be lucky to match the overall performance of the stock market. In the course of a decade, 75% of all stock funds underperform the market. There are reasons why most investors do poorly. Nearly all center on the notion that individual investors are overconfident about their own abilities. When Statman and Shefrin studied the returns of a large discount brokerage firm, 15% of the gains were realized, while only 10% of losses were.

Even though the losses could be written off on taxes.

People were much more willing to sell good stocks and keep the dogs. There was a real hesitancy toward selling bad investments.

When I was a stockbroker in 1981, one client became ecstatic when a stock he owned increased even 5%. He'd almost break out the champagne. Heaven forbid, if the stock did even better, he would immediately tell me to sell and take the profit. This same emotional investor would call many times a day complaining when an investment lost money. The conversation was usually not whether the stock was appropriate for his portfolio. Instead it was centered on whether it would move back into positive territory and when.

TWENTY-EIGHT
Benefectance (Hero to Zero Effect)

People tend to view success as a result of their own action, and failure due to factors largely outside their control. If my portfolio makes money, it is because I am diligent in investing. If it loses money, it means I received bad advice.

There's a term for those people who think good things are a result of their own abilities and bad outcomes are due to the advice of others. It's called "Benefectance," or the "Hero to Zero Effect."

One reason for this is people think so highly of themselves they often won't accept responsibility for mistakes, or accept they could be wrong. So the blame is transferred to others, especially a paid financial advisor, when poor outcomes occur. In the 1970s, I played tennis tournaments in Europe. Today tennis is still

> *"I'm a genius if it works. It's your fault if it doesn't"*

my favorite sport. John McEnroe came on the scene about 1981, teaching a whole new generation of players that misbehaving was a good way of providing distraction during a match. It was not very sportsmanlike, but the worse he played, the more he would blame the line judges and umpire for any infraction, no matter how minor. He would even blame the photographers for clicking too loudly.

Recently I saw a match between tennis legends Bjorn Borg and McEnroe.

"Johnny Mac" had missed an easy forehand and immediately started to berate the line judge for his poor eyesight. It's also a safe bet if Johnny Mac was playing at the peak of his game, he would not congratulate the same line judge on his accuracy.

It never ceases to amaze when faced with a foolish decision, people will invariably explain away the poor "Wisdom and success come from experience.

Experience comes from mistakes. The more mistakes you make, the more wisdom and success you will have" outcome as bad luck, bad timing, or somebody else's fault. When things go well, it's because of their super ability. Psychological researcher Martin Seligman refers to this behavior as "Learned Helplessness." In order to stay confident, according to Seligman, people need to blame bad things on others, but this also prevents us from learning the right lessons from our mistakes.

There are three types of Hero to Zero effects:

1. **The Illusion of Control**: Overconfident investors think they can control even uncontrollable events.

2. **Self-Attribution Bias**: Investors believe success comes from their own ability and failure comes as a result of bad luck and/or bad advice from others.

3. **Hindsight Bias**: They convince themselves after the fact that more attention paid to their gut would have prevented the mistake in the first place.

I'm an author, speaker, and a business coach. We promise our clients an increase in business by 80% within eight weeks through one-on-one coaching.

Most of our clients stay two or three years in coaching despite the minimal requirement of six months. It's wonderful to see the client, whether an owner or salesperson, grow their business so quickly. But these remarkably successful people rarely attribute their good fortune to coaching. A fairly typical example is Pat. She doubled her business within six months. She was so successful so fast that she was asked by her company to give the keynote speech during their national convention.

They all wanted to know her fast start secrets.

She spent 45 minutes on stage talking about the techniques we worked on together yielding remarkable success.

But never once did Pat mention where she learned her techniques or who helped her stay on track. I asked if she mentioned me in the program. She forgot.

This is a very good example of the Hero to Zero effect.

If you fall victim, you will repeat the same mistakes over and over again, attributing poor results to bad luck or others' mistakes. Above all, be humble. Success is never forever and failure is never fatal. A sage once said, "Wisdom and success come from experience. Experience comes from mistakes. The more mistakes you make, the more wisdom and success you will have."

TWENTY-NINE
Projection Bias

When you have a tough time financially, you are likely to say, "The economy is difficult for everybody." If you don't like the cold weather, you suggest, "Nobody does." In other words, the way we feel and act is projected to others by how we see the world.

The same thing may true of the attitude you possess as you invest. "Projection Bias" may cause you to believe in the constancy of what you have experienced.

> *"The way I see the world is the way it really is"*

The return of investments you currently have will perform much the same way in the future. This may also cause you to keep bad investments too long or sell good ones too soon.

Projection Bias can also be a mental weight in financial planning. As we plan for retirement, it's difficult to imagine a life different than our current experience. When my daughters were in high school, there was a lot of stress in monitoring their parties and friends. I would constantly worry they would meet boys that were the way I was at their age. I often projected the worst in the boys they liked. It was hard to imagine college would be much different.

All in all, Projection Bias overemphasizes our current experience and is an indicator of what is likely to happen in the future. In the Great Recession of 2007–2009, the stock market dropped like a rock by 54%.

Many investors bailed out, thinking it would only continue to lose. In the midst of all this was a roller coaster level of volatility. Many retirees know that a certain portion of investments should be guaranteed. As you grow older, that portion also should increase. But thinking about the market in terms of Projection Bias would be an investor psychology weakness. It may prohibit you from seeing an investment objectively instead of through the filter of your own emotion.

THIRTY
Framing

It's really not what you say; it's how you say it. If a choice is framed in a certain way, it will influence your decision. When credit cards were first introduced, banks were faced with a public used to paying in cash. Banks made their money not just on the big purchases, but on small transactions as well. Merchants, in the beginning, were loathe to accepting credit cards since they had to pay a fee. So a brilliant marketer came up with the term "discount fee" to make it all more palatable. Actually, in the beginning, it was called a "cash discount." How is that for confusing?

"Since you put it that way"

This ploy is also used in politics. Estate taxes have been reframed as "The Death Tax." Who could be for a tax at death? The flat tax, favored by conservatives, has been framed as the "The Fair Tax." Again, who couldn't support a fairer tax? Political pollster Frank

Luntz, in his book, Words that Work, believes anything can be accepted or rejected if is framed properly.

During the mid-term elections of 2010, Republicans staged a congressional sweep of 64 seats. Republicans tried to frame Democrats as "tax and spend socialists."

The Democrats attempted to frame conservative Tea Party candidates as extremists. This shouldn't be an influence, but we are influenced by how arguments are framed and often make decisions based on that structure.

In 1981, "Science" journal featured a paper titled "The Framing of Decisions and the Psychology of Choice," written by Tversky and Kahneman. They offered an unusual Asian disease expected to kill 600 people.

Two alternative programs were proposed. If the subject chose program A, there would be a projected 200 people saved, but if one chose program B, there would be a one-third chance that 600 people would be saved and two-thirds chance that no one would be saved. The authors found 72% of the respondents chose program A, although the outcomes of both programs were identical. They surmised most people are risk averse.

Then Tversky and Kahneman reframed the problem.

This time they suggested program C: 400 people would die and with program D, a one-third probability no one would die and a two-thirds probability that 600 would die. Reframing in this way, 78% chose program D although both outcomes were again identical. However, the first scenario was framed in terms of lives saved and the second framed

"We tend to react to adverse information more readily than positive information"

as lived lost. We tend to react to adverse information more readily than positive information.

Perhaps this is why negative political ads are so abhorred, yet so effective. Everyone complains about dirty political campaigns, yet the mud continues to be slung.

How a decision is framed has an impact on your investment choice. You are informed there is a 40% chance of a 10% market correction next year and a 60% chance the market will continue to increase. You are more likely to react to the chance of losing money that you are to the status quo. This goes deeper than just reacting to fear. It is about how the choice is framed. I remember a political speaker recently saying the election is about whether you want to take your government back or give up control to the special interest groups. It doesn't seem like this kind of argument would work. But it does. Can't people think of more than just those two alternatives? It's all about how the questions are framed.

THIRTY-ONE
Bandwagon Effect

When I was a stockbroker with Kidder Peabody in Newport Beach, CA, there was a shoe shine guy in the lobby. He was an amateur investor yet very savvy.

Mike would tell me what stocks he liked and which he was selling that day. He liked working in our building because he got so many great stock ideas. He shined my shoes everyday not because they were dirty or I was particularly vain, I just wanted to hear what the common investor was buying so I could sell my clients out of those positions.

"It must be true because everyone says so"

It's hard to make sense of all the information we are bombarded with. We listen and watch more than 3,000 pieces of TV, radio, billboard, newspaper, and internet ads on a daily basis. And these are just the advertisements.

Stories without solicitations add an extra 30%. From all this, we only retain seven items after one day, three impressions after two days and none after one week. When I finish a new book, my publishers tell me it takes seven exposures to get enough interest from people to actually buy it.

This deluge of data is called an "Information Cascade."

It causes a desensitization glaze of too much information.

Essentially, the information cascade theory suggests popular trends or fads begin when investors ignore common sense and focus instead on the popular opinions of others. The actions of a herd are even more persuasive than an investors own instinct, common sense, and personal knowledge. This is kind of like a traffic jam on a freeway. As one car brakes to avoid the car in front, it causes the cars behind to brake at the same place jamming the freeway for the next few hours.

Recently my flight to Chicago was delayed due to yet one more mechanical problem. When I fly, I have a rule of getting off any airplane I am on with mechanical problems.

I have been stranded too many times while the airline "incrementalizes" the delay promising status reports in ten minutes, then 30 minutes, and so on. Usually, after a few hours, the airline eventually cancels the flight. During one trip, the pilot taxied out to the runway and then back to the gate. He waited for nearly 30 minutes before he told passengers there was a problem with the right engine. As soon as we pulled up to the gate, I immediately got up, pulled off my two bags and walked off the airplane. As I stood up from my seat, nearly 25% of the passengers also stood up. The flight attendant had to beg the passengers on the intercom to stay seated. They were all reacting to one person leaving the airplane.

So we tend to go along with the herd. The problem is the investment herd is eventually always wrong. If you are at the end of a trend, there is a great chance you will lose money. As the old says goes, "When chased by a

> *"When chased by a bear, I only have to run faster than you"*

bear, I only have to run slightly faster than you." All bubbles are driven by herding instinct. By the time you hear a trend has started, it's too late to make any money. One of my poker buddies once said, "If you can't spot the sucker at the table, it's you."

During one CNBC investment analysis program, three of the four panelists recommended buying oil.

They all agreed oil would go 10% higher in the next few weeks. They actually had some great expert analysis to back up their views. They quoted currencies swings and shortages. Yet over the next few weeks, oil actually decreased in value by 15% based on seasonal shortages. Those who bought based on the herd's congruence lost money.

People tend to believe that something is a better idea if a lot of other people are doing it. In essence, they are trying to gain a free ride on the analysis of others.

Many assume, "Someone must have thought this thing out." The Bandwagon Effect has its uses; we don't all need to learn every hard lesson ourselves. But when herding behavior is produced, market swings become more pronounced as more and more people enter each bubble, and consequently lose money. In other words, we get booms and busts. A financial advisor is less likely to get fired by his client if the herd also loses money.

Some neuro-economic studies have shown the brain actually secretes a chemical to the pre-frontal cortex creating discomfort when you are forced to go against the crowd. In one study of vertical lines, researcher Solomon Asch offered three choices to match a sample. Though only one line was a match, 32% picked the obvious wrong answer when participants were planted to sway the truth, even when the correct answer was in black and white.

The Bandwagon Effect has an impact on investment behavior because it's easier to follow the majority than think for ourselves. It is very difficult to go against the conventional wisdom when everyone is saying the same thing. Yet this is how investors lose their entire nest eggs.

A teacher who inherited some assets decided to retire.

In 1997, the teacher and spouse wanted to sell all their real estate holdings and go "all in" during the tech bubble. Their financial advisor Scott tried to convince the clients that it was wrong to put their nest egg of $2 Million into tech instead of being well diversified.

The clients were adamant and when Scott refused to support their irrational decision, a 20 year relationship was put into jeopardy. The clients finally relented only to watch the market go down 40% in 2001. Then again in 2005, the same clients wanted to go "all in" on real estate thinking the real money was not in equities, but in property. Again Scott intervened and told the clients to stay diversified. The clients again threatened to leave Scott for a more compliant advisor. Finally, the clients stayed put and saved another major loss of 45% of their portfolio. If the clients followed their irrational temptation to follow the herd at any point over that ten year period, they would have lost 75% of their $2 Million retirement.

In one study by Dalbar Research, annual investor returns from 1990–2009 would have been 8.2% if an investor only followed the

S&P index. But the average investor instead made a return of only 3.17%. Much of this was due to the Bandwagon Effect.

In 1996, an obscure Canadian mining company started to broadcast a major gold discovery at a jungle site on the Indonesian island of Borneo. Soon the stock shot up from $2 per share in 1995 to $19.50 per share in September of 1996. There was a chance thousands of investors understood the gold mining business well enough to recognize the company, Bre-X, was a good buy and the claims were truthful. More likely though, a small number of investors enticed even more investors to jump in on all the fun and capital gains.

Soon Bre-X's senior executives sold off their shares at vastly inflated prices. It soon became apparent also that Bre-X was a pyramid scheme. If you were late to this party, you lost a lot of money. In early 1997, independent analysis revealed that Bre-X's claims were unfounded.

The senior managers were soon prosecuted for stock fraud. Bre-X's stock value became worthless.

But this is how herding behavior works. Very few are willing, or sometimes even capable of putting in the hours of due diligence to make sure an investment is appropriate and valuable.

In one study by Harvard psychologist Paul Andreassen, investors who received no news performed better than those who paid attention to a constant stream of information; good or bad. He studied groups of engaged versus disinterested investors. Paying attention to the stock prices of real companies and real news reports, two of the groups made decisions about a relatively stable stock. One group was subjected to constant news reports about a company while the other received no news at all. The same test was given to two other groups. This company stock was subject to wider price swings than the previous company. Investors in this study who received no news saw higher returns than those who received a constant stream of information.

The investors trading in the more volatile stock earned more than twice as much, as long as they were insulated from news.

On May 6, 2010, the stock market dropped by almost 800 points within a few hours. The rumor was a broker trading Proctor and Gamble stock pushed the B (billion) button instead of the M (million) button entering a sell order for a client. Because more than 70% of market trades are done now by computerized trading systems, a sell order of 1 billion shares was immediately interpreted by these programmed trading platforms to be a market sell-off fueled by still more herding behavior. Since computers are programmed by human beings, herding behavior is now hardwired into computer software. The Bandwagon Effect is apparently difficult to escape.

THIRTY-TWO
Instant Gratification

It should be increasingly apparent that a small reward today is worth a lot more than great success tomorrow.

This "Instant Gratification" is an obvious driver in young children. If they can't get what they want right now, a temper tantrum with the trappings of crying and stomping will ensue until they get it. Very few of us believe the same behavior is prevalent in adults. But consider this, if someone sends you a critical e-mail, your first impulse is to defend yourself and attack them in return. During a dream car test drive, you start to negotiate a price with the salesperson as soon as you park.

Robert Cialdini, in his book, Influence, tells the story of one commodities broker who cold-called a prospect. The salesperson explained he was not trying to sell anything, instead he was just asking if the pros-

> "Cooking a turkey in an 'I want it now' TV dinner world"

134 Why Smart People Make Dumb Mistakes With Their Money

pect was interested in hearing about any good investment ideas in the future. The prospective investor said yes. A week later the broker called saying he had not yet found anything good but would keep looking.

A week later he called again with pandemonium in the background. He said the market was exploding. Soybeans were going through the roof. It was important to get in fast or lose the opportunity. The prospect, already on the hook, felt compelled to act instantly and lost money as a result. Waiting doesn't have the same psychological reward of instant gratification; however, whenever you feel compelled to act on an offer quickly, it's just like the child who can't get his way.

Harvard behavioral economist David Laibson created a formal model that describes the Instant Gratification dynamic. He discussed starting an exercise program, entailing an immediate cost of six units of value. But this program would create a delayed benefit of eight units. One who was willing to postpone the immediate gain would net two units. It seems obvious that any rational person would wait. But logic ignores the human tendency to devalue the future in favor of the present, according to Laibson. The notion is we spend too much for a desire now rather than defer for bigger rewards in the future. We buy things we can't afford on a credit card, diminishing our ability for more comfort later. In most cases, considering rational decision making, there seems to be a two to one trade off. I will avoid spending $100 today as long as I can receive $200 within the very near future. The smaller the return and the longer the waiting period, the less likely I am to act in my own best interest. So it seems that a bird in the hand is actually much more highly valued than two in the bush.

One financial advisor talks about curing credit card spending with the "Ice Glass Method." This is sort of a home remedy for impulsive spending. You put your credit card into a glass of water and then into a freezer.

When you impulsively decide to make a purchase, you are then required to first wait for the ice to thaw before using the credit card to make a purchase. By then, the Instant Gratification impulse has worn off, forcing you to make a more considered buy.

THIRTY-THREE
Procrastination

We promise to save our money, but don't. We commit to exercise and lose weight, but instead gain by not signing up for a gym membership. One of the biggest headwinds to your investment success is your tendency to procrastinate. You fill out your federal tax returns on April 14, sometimes making mistakes in the process. You pay property taxes a day before they are due, at times incurring a penalty. We miss deadlines insuring a needless cost. All because we put off today what we think we can accomplish tomorrow.

"I want to put off today what I can do tomorrow"

Many years ago, Ford Motor Company tried to get car owners into dealerships for routine maintenance.

Even with warranty service, dealerships make a lot of money. Part of the problem was Ford's average car had 18,000 parts requiring service, with 20 different vehicle types. Some parts need to be serviced at 3,600 miles while others at 4,200 miles and so on. This became so complex, not only for customers, but also dealership workers became confused. Honda had a new idea.

Honda vehicles also have 18,000 parts in many different models. But instead of Ford, all maintenance was lumped into three schedules: 5,000, 10,000 and 20,000 mile intervals. Customers at Honda were no longer confused and complied more frequently. Once Ford copied the Honda service model, bays once 40% vacant, were soon full.

One way to avoid procrastination is to take away the opportunity of "later." Since later never comes, anything you choose not to do now, you must decide never to do. This may be easier said than done. If you're organized and decide on an activity, you need to decide that anything not written in your calendar now will never be accomplished. It's easier to say no, knowing if you don't take action the moment you hear it, you will never do it. But everything falls apart if you don't have the discipline to stay with your schedule.

This "default to decision" concept will be a good start on avoiding procrastination.

THIRTY-FOUR
Decision Paralysis

D ecision Paralysis" is caused by too much information and often, too many choices. It's much easier to choose between two options than 100. It's easier to choose between cable TV and DirecTV, between a BMW and Mercedes, or between chicken and steak. Restaurateurs have long known the bigger the menu, the more likely customers are to order a simple soup or salad.

> *"The more I hear, the more paralyzed I get"*

Decision Paralysis occurs when there is so much to think about that I will do nothing. There are several symptoms for Decision Paralysis:

1. Can't choose between investment options.
2. Don't contribute to pension plans at work.
3. Delay making investment or spending decisions.

In one study done by Stanford researchers Sheena Sethi and Mark Lepper, buyers in a Menlo Park, California upscale grocery were exposed to jams. 30% of those shown six jams made a purchase versus only 3% who viewed 24 jams. A lot of choice doesn't seem to help us make better decisions, it causes paralysis. One reason why mortgage companies and utilities want to direct deduct from your bank account is decision paralysis, procrastination, instant gratification, and loss aversion all rolled into one. If a mortgage bill comes and you have to decide whether to repair the fridge or save for a new car, you might be tempted to postpone the mortgage payment. If your electric bill comes, you may be tempted to go out to dinner that night, buy a new jacket, or new tires for your aging 12-year-old clunker. The direct deduction vendors want to take your decision out of the mix. Of course you can always stop the payment process, but that would take a decision "not" to make the mortgage payment. It's the decision that is the hard part.

Dan Ariely, in his book, Predictably Irrational, describes a 2010 B.C. Chinese commander named Xiang Yu. Xiang led his troops across the Yangtze River to attack the army of the Chin Dynasty. While camping on the banks for the night, his troops woke up to discover their ships were burning. The troops hurried to fight off the attackers but soon realized it was Xiang Yu himself who set the ships on fire. He also ordered all the cooking pots crushed. The commander then announced without pots and ships, the troops had no choice but to fight their way to victory or perish. They fought ferociously against a larger enemy, winning the next nine consecutive battles obliterating the main force of the Chin Dynasty.

We would never think of limiting our options, but because we have so many, confusion often causes us to use none. If we lose the next battle, we can always take the ship home. If we don't win, we can walk back to the cooking pots knowing there is a meal waiting.

Welterweight boxing champion Manny "Pac-Man" Pacquiao grew up in a poor Philippines village. Part of a large family with a single mother, he had no option except to fend for himself. Finding a dilapidated boxing gym when he was nine years old, Pacquiao trained constantly for hours preparing daily for his first bout.

Hard work paid off. In time, he would make millions of dollars. In 2010, he was even elected to political office in the Philippines. If you had no option in life except to succeed, it's likely the lack of choice would make you think about the future differently.

Jason Zweig of "Money" magazine said, "It is better to make bad decisions with your money than make no decisions at all." As explained earlier, dollar cost averaging is a good way to keep investing on a constant basis, minimizing the need for investment decisions."

THIRTY-FIVE
Reversion To The Mean

Investors are famously off the mark when assessing stock value and market direction on a day-to-day, or even year-to-year basis. University of Chicago's Richard Thaler and Werner De Bondt of the University of Wisconsin analyzed the performance of stocks on the New York Stock Exchange. They examined stocks that either moved up or down in excess of their average share. Then they examined six-year tenure blocks of time and divided those periods in half. Returns from the first period were called the "formation period." Stock performance over the second half of the study was called the "holding period." They discovered extreme returns were often followed by a significant price movement in the opposite direction. Simply, they discovered stocks whose prices bounced up or down would likely be reversed over time.

"What goes up must come down"

Those who trade depending on this prediction are called "Contrarian Investors." Contrarians love to evaluate the market as too optimistic or pessimistic. When there is euphoria and common investors seem excited about the future, contrarians tend to sell. When investors seem the most pessimistic, for example in March of 2009, contrarians tend to buy. If you sold your investments on March 8, 2009, you would have lost 54% of your money during the great recession starting in 2007. But, if you bought stocks on March 8, 2009, when everybody else was the most pessimistic, you would've been rewarded with a stock price run-up of 48%.

Experienced investors look at each stock's resistance and support levels over a period of time. Over six months they measure the support lows as well as the resistance highs. If the stock moves up through the resistance level, a good investor will sell, sensing a reversion back to its moving average. As a stock dips below its support level, a good investor will buy, knowing the stock will revert higher again to its average.

A hot new restaurant in town has an hour wait to get in. Curious diners are willing to take the extra time curious to check it out. The food is good, but not that great. The next time they visit, the wait is just as long.

When the company's IPO is released to the market, the description is very exciting and draws hundreds of millions of dollars in investment, but then drops like a rock. The reason for the stock drop is customer service at the restaurant chain is poor. Waiting an hour is not worth it. So a popular restaurant reverts back to the mean because it can't handle the extra customers.

This is a good example of why companies are often unable to cope with too much business, and why many potentially great companies become only good when they revert to the average. An exception would be Starbucks coffee. I personally am not willing to wait 30 minutes for a cup of coffee at an airport. I would much rather buy a cup immediately at another vendor for half the price. But for some reason, Starbucks customers are willing to put up with the wait making Starbucks unlikely to revert to the average.

THIRTY-SIX
Snakebite Bias

If you have ever made an investment that failed, as all of us have, you may be gun shy, avoiding that same asset class in the future. In extreme cases you may avoid investing at all. This is called "Snakebite Bias."

If you invested in a particular mutual fund dropping 55% during the great recession of 2008, you may be unlikely to put more money into it today.

There once was a blacksmith who made horseshoes by bending red-hot metal into a semi-circle and hammering the forms into horseshoes. One day, a young boy named Ben was talking to the black-smith. He picked up a hot horseshoe and immediately dropped it into the bucket of water. The blacksmith then said, "Did that burn you son?" The boy then replied, "No sir, it just doesn't take me long to look at a horseshoe."

> "Boy, I will never do that again"

The same is true today for certain classes of investments.

Annuities would never be considered by some investors because of bad experiences. Annuities are often wonderful fixed investments if sold by a reputable broker and positioned well in a portfolio.

Snakebite Bias against annuities may be an investment decision mistake.

Snakebite Bias often is a result of a broad-based effect of past events. Often culminating in loss aversion, these individual investments, or classes of investments, can influence future behavior. Debbie had invested for ten years in the stock market. She invested most of her retirement savings of $200,000 in an equity mutual fund. Two years after her initial investment, the value of the fund fell to $150,000. She sold her stocks during a temporary dip in the market. But because of Snakebite Bias, she has kept her retirement in CDs ever since. Even now, she refuses to invest in stocks, often telling her friends stocks are way too risky. Because of this bias, Debbie is doomed to returns that barely keep up with inflation and may even lose money after taxes.

THIRTY-SEVEN
Cognitive Dissonance

When investors evaluate conflicting information, they tend to develop a bias toward one and rationalize why they made it. They may even dismiss opposing information.

"Cognitive Dissonance" may be the reason why investors make very poor decisions with contradictory ideas. The market had been depressed for the last year, yet an advisor recommends putting more money in thinking stocks are undervalued and it's time for a rebound. Cognitive Dissonance rests in the avoidance of greater losses versus the desire to capitalize on a pending market increase.

Your ability to avoid Cognitive Dissonance may also rest in your level of confidence. An investor with high self-esteem might recognize this is an opportunity to recover some losses;

"All this thinking gives me a headache"

whereas one with a poor self-perception may want to take money out thinking they can never beat the market, so why try?

Symptoms of Cognitive Dissonance are: procrastination, loss aversion, and status quo bias. You are much more likely to stay with what you have when faced with conflicting information. One investor went to a seminar put on by an advisor recommending safety in retirement. But transferring their assets into a safe investment would cause them to terminate a relationship with a broker they've used for the last ten years. Moving the money seemed to be the right thing to do, but caused emotional conflict. They would have to face the broker. One couple actually told an advisor they did not want to move their money because they didn't want to end the relationship, even though the current broker was doing them no good.

Cognitive Dissonance also causes us to make the same mistakes over and over again. One of my friends is very cheap. He knows that continually trying to get a discount causes him to buy sub-standard products that don't last. He knows purchasing better made brand name products will last longer. But his temptation to save money often is in conflict with his desire to avoid having to continually replace what he bought.

My friend Anthony Parinello sold computers for Hewlett-Packard many years ago. San Diego State University assembled all the major manufacturers asking for the lowest price for a campus-wide mainframe.

When Tony started to walk out of the room, the provost of the university asked why he was leaving.

Tony said, "All you're looking for is the lowest price. You need to be evaluating the overall cost." The provost then asked what the difference was. Tony replied, "Price is what you pay right now, cost is what you pay over the long run." This is the type of clearheaded thinking Cognitive Dissonance sufferers struggle with.

Confusion creates emotional insecurity. And rather than make a logical decision, they tend to make no decisions at all.

THIRTY-EIGHT
How Do I Turn Bias into Profit?

A lot of research shows investors tend to exit or enter the market at exactly the wrong times. They often buy right after a dramatic increase in market value and sell after a substantial stock market decrease. Warren Buffett once said contrarian investing is always the right path. Being greedy when others are fearful, and fearful when others are greedy is extremely difficult, no matter who you are. If you decide to use a financial advisor, rationally tell the planner to be assertive in defending his recommendations. Let him know that you value his advice. But you will be emotional and sometimes even tell the advisor what portfolio changes to make.

You will often be wrong.

This is the start of a mature investment mindset.

You are emotionally attached to your money and will usually make the wrong decisions. But your financial advisor is focused on your goals instead of your emotions.

A good advisor will be supportive, but also cogently advise a non-emotional path.

One of my financial advisor coaching clients once told me a story of one of his clients, who lost nearly 45% of their assets in 2008. In February 2009, the client lost so much of their retirement, they were frightened about running out of money during their later years. The financial advisor told him the portfolio was well diversified and balanced. The portfolio was based on the rule of 100, meaning that the age of the client was in safe investments and the balance from their age to 100 was in more risky equities. The adviser knew the market would come back. If the investments did not recover, there would be bigger fish to fry, meaning the US economy would never recover as well.

The client insisted on taking all their money out of the stock market, but the financial advisor held his ground.

It would've been very easy for an advisor to just execute the client's wishes. But the client was acting emotionally while the advisor focused on investment goals and past stock market behavior. He told his client if they wanted to sell their positions, they would also have to look for a new financial advisor. After a display of more emotion, the client backed off. It was a good thing he did. On March 9 of 2009, the market recovered bouncing to a 26% return for the rest of the year. Acting emotionally is always a bad idea.

Another idea is to turn off the TV. Financial shows like CNBC, Bloomberg, and Fox Business, are what one of my clients call, financial pornography. They make their money by sensationalism to boost ratings hour by hour. They often pump up stories that will only scare their viewers into making financial mistakes.

But a great financial advisor will call you every few months, giving you a market update. This will add context to the day-to-day craziness you will hear as an investor. Most of the sharpest brokers know that company earnings drive the stock market. Yet when CNBC talks about economic issues in Europe, slow growth in China, and a well known company taking a fall because of poor accounting procedures, it makes viewers think they should sell their investments and wait for calmer waters. But that is what these channels will communicate every day. Turn off the TV, and call your advisor. She will help you keep your emotional head on straight Investment Cycle Emotion

There are two cycles critical in making any investments.

One is the Business Cycle, and the other the Sentiment Cycle. Like a rising curve, the Business Cycle starts with movement to a peak followed by a downward slope towards recession. This is followed by a trough at the bottom moving again up to expansion as the cycle repeats. Both of these cycles are in the study guide included in this program.

The Sentiment Cycle follows the same curve. It starts with optimism, moving up to excitement, moving up to thrill, then higher to euphoria. After that, the downward part of the curve starts with anxiety moving down to denial, further down to fear, followed by desperation, moving down to panic, further to capitulation, bottoming out with despondency, and depression.

That bottoming process then starts an upward slope to hope, relief, and optimism starting the cycle over again.

While wrongheaded emotional decisions can be made at any part in the curve, the worst decisions are usually made at desperation, panic, capitulation, despondency and depression.

As the Business Cycle moves down past recession, settling on the trough, experienced investors buy. Because they know emotional investors during that part of the business cycle will feel fear, desperation, panic, capitulation, despondency, and depression. This is where expert, professional investors gain their biggest returns. But the opposite is true at the top of the Business Cycle curve. Starting with the upward movement of expansion, followed by the peak, gives expert investors a signal to sell. Experts know emotional investors will feel optimism, excitement, thrill, followed by euphoria at the top.

Before Federal Reserve Chairman Ben Bernanke, was Federal Reserve Chairman Alan Greenspan.

Greenspan called the euphoria peak, irrational exuberance.

He was aware of how emotional investors would invest in and create bubbles followed by panic when the bubbles burst.

One of the symptoms of the Business, Sentiment cycle is Herd behavior. We discussed this earlier, but in the 1990s and early 2000's, approximately $18 billion of new assets moved into domestic growth equities because of investor enthusiasm for the tech industry.

Three years before the peak levels, US large-cap growth stocks had returned 14% and had outperformed global equities by almost four percentage points per year. One of the mistakes investors made was another emotional mistake, called Representative Bias. This means that people have a tendency to predict future returns based on past and current returns. Many investors thought the high domestic growth technology industry returns, would continue for many years in the future. Shortly after, dot.com tech bubble burst, wiping out many portfolios. According to MorningStar reports in 2009, mutual funds with the greatest inflows tended to under-perform those with the greatest outflows over the following three and five year periods.

With this all means is when investors perceive risk, they become risk-averse at the wrong time and lower their equity positions decreasing their chances for long-term wealth. Greg Fisher, chief investment officer for Gerstein-Fisher once said, "We don't have people with investment problems, we have investments with people problems."

Rebalancing your investments Another mistake emotional investors make, is failing to rebalance their portfolios. It's important to weight a portfolio depending on your age, investment goals, and risk. This means that as an investment gains

"We don't have people with investment problems, we have investments with people problems."

value, it commands a greater proportion of money, or weight, in your portfolio. When this happens, your portfolio becomes out of balance, causing your overall investment basket to become overly sensitive to market fluctuation.

We discussed Prospect Theory earlier. This is when you sell good investments and keep the bad. But rebalancing means your portfolio needs to maintain balance between stocks, bonds, treasuries, and other asset classes. And within the stock portion of your portfolio, a balance needs to be maintained between growth, value, small-cap, large-cap, and other sectors. If you are managing your investments on your own, rebalancing should be done every three months.

We also discussed Status Quo Bias. With respect to rebalancing, there's a tendency to set and forget. Status Quo Bias causes you to avoid change. Rebalancing by definition is change. But you need change to make sure your portfolio does not become too volatile. This is one more reason why investing on your own may not be a good idea. The discipline and emotional detachment required is too much for most individual investors.

In 2006, before the Great Recession, I was invested nearly 90% in equities. I had a balance between Large-Cap, Small-Cap, Value, and Growth. The S&P decreased by 45%, and my losses completely mirrored the market except for the 10% of my portfolio held in cash. I was 54 years old, and should have kept at least 50% of my investments fixed or in asset classes that could not go down, like annuities. In January 2009, at exactly the wrong time, I put 10% of my portfolio into annuities. About three years late. This is just one more example of how, even those of us who think we know what we are doing, make serious mistakes.

I've also talked about Home Bias, your tendency to invest in what you know the best and are closest to.

For example, someone who works at a Wall Street stock brokerage will likely overweight equities. Someone who works at a real estate company will be tempted to put too much money in real estate. One GM retiree put nearly 80% of his investments in GM right before its bankruptcy. You will be very tempted to overweight investments that you are loyal to. But it's critical that you balance your portfolio appropriately.

The Cost of Income

Another mistake in your portfolio is trying to get income from asset classes like annuities. For example, a company may offer 6% income on your investment.

But that 6% may come at a high cost. Often your quest for income may cost you an extra 1% fee. Find out how much an income rider will cost. It may be better to take income from selling equities or buying bonds. But even then, high yield bonds are closely correlated with preferred stocks. This means, as the stock market becomes volatile, bonds will react in the same way. It could be better to sell equities for income in part of your portfolio than to buy an investment that throws off monthly income.

The Impact of Inflation

Inflation is another risk that most investors ignore.

Historically inflation has been between 2.5% and 4%.

In fact the government will adjust Social Security payments based on the government produced statistic called the cost-of-living index. But if you have gone to a grocery store to buy milk, meat, or even produce, or pretty much anything you need not measured by the cost of living index, you know the government inflation rate is dramatically underestimated.

Inflation is very bad for your retirement. A retirement account with $100,000 today may be worth only $50,000 in buying power in 10 years. When I was in business school getting my MBA, we were expected to calculate net present value of investments calculating the value today of an investment versus 10 years in the future. But a simpler explanation is a movie I watched a few nights ago shot in 1984. The actor walked into a pizza store and ordered a pepperoni pizza for $3.50.

The last time I looked at pizza online, it was $12 with only one topping. Over 30 years from 1984 to 2014 the price of pizza in a very unscientific example quadrupled. The same thing will happen to your retirement portfolio. Make sure that any plans you make also have an inflation calculation for buying power over the next 10 to 30 years. The last thing you want is to have only enough money for rent and food but nothing else.

It's also very interesting to see bank advertisements for CDs. From 2009 until 2014, rates were advertised at less than 2%. If you wanted to tie your money up for five years, you might be able to get 2.5%. But inflation is historically much higher. And real inflation for the things you buy is between 5% and 10%. Yet most people are financially illiterate. They think the only safe investment is money in a bank. While this is true for only $100,000, with an FDIC government increase slightly later, you are actually losing money after inflation. Any money past the FDIC guarantee is at risk. A bank CD is only a slightly better investment than keeping your money in a mattress. At least in a bank, your money is better protected.

This is particularly bad for seniors with fixed incomes.

There's a natural tendency to keep your money safe when retired. Yet, if you don't make the right inflation considered, retirement financial decisions, you will lose money every month.

The Impact of Taxes

Another big mistake investors make is not recognizing the cost of taxes in their portfolio. Even 85% of your social security can be taxed if you make more than $40,000 per year per 2014 rules. This is totally unfair since you already paid into the Social Security system during your work years. But the government can change taxes on your retirement anytime they want.

The latest ideas floated are means testing Social Security.

If you make more than $100,000 a year, or have more than $1 million in retirement assets, the government may take Social Security away from you completely.

The system currently is projected to run out of money by 2033 unless they make dramatic changes.

Those changes may mean that your payments are severely decreased or that you could be excluded from Social Security completely.

Another tax consideration is investment returns.

You should focus more on after-tax investment return and then on stated returns. Capital Gains tax is a moving object. Depending on who is in power running the government, it may move from 15% to as high as 35%, and change at any time. You already know that income tax is progressive. For example, making even $1,000 more per year can put you into a higher tax bracket. This may even cause you to reject a job promotion.

But the same is true with your investments.

In one study, it was shown that effective tax planning can add up to 1% higher return on your investments.

So whether you are working with a financial advisor, or on your own, look at returns on an after-tax basis.

One formula that nearly every financial advisor uses is the rule of 72. This is a measurement that considers compounding when calculating investment return. Albert Einstein once said that compounding is one of the wonders of the universe. Compounding starts with say, 10% return on $10, which gives you a one dollar return over the next year. But a 10% return on the following year would not be based on your $10 investment, it is based on the total return plus original investment of $11, times another 10% equaling $12.21 and so on for every year that you get a 10% return.

The Rule of 72

So would you like to learn how long it takes to double your money due to compounding? The Rule of 72 will show you how. Just take 72 divided by the interest percentage per year to find out the approximate number of years it will take to double your investment. For example, if you get an interest rate of 6%, it will take 12 years to double your money. But an interest or investment return rate of 12% annually will take only six years to double your money, because of compounding.

This is a really useful tool in estimating how much money you will have over 10, 20 and even 30 years, as long as you can estimate your investment rate of return.

A rule of thumb is to use a return of 7.25 for the stock market. In the last 60 years the US stock market has returned about 7.25%. So a realistic example is a portfolio of $100,000 invested in the stock market.

The Rule of 72 states that your investment would grow to $200,000 in just short of 10 years. But don't forget taxes and inflation. That may put a damper on your enthusiasm, or what Alan Greenspan once said, "Irrational Exuberance."

Dollar Cost Averaging

Here's a question for you. Can you get a better return by putting all your money into the market? Or doing it little by little? The answer may be Dollar Cost Averaging.

This is a very popular technique used by both institutional pension investors as well as individuals.

In this strategy, you gradually invest money in the stock market in monthly increments, instead of one lump sum. In one study, it was shown that lump-sum investing was better when the markets had capitulated, or at a bottom. But unless you know when markets are bottoming, investing in monthly increments is probably safer. One of my clients uses a strategy called Scaling.

Or taking a lump sum and investing in equal amounts every month over a 1 year period.

In this case, you are buying more shares when prices are low, and less shares when prices are high. In one Prudential insurance retirement commercial recently, an economics professor asked people on the street how much money they had in their pockets.

Most people had between $5 and $40. He then asked who could retire on that money? All said no. Then the camera panned to building blocks in a park starting with a small block of $10 ending with a huge block of $100,000 at the end. Like dominoes, the small $10 block was pushed down cascading to the hundred thousand dollar block eventually falling. TV commercials are written for a 12th grade education. But you and I both know that the strategy to achieve this increase is really just Dollar Cost Averaging. Contributing $10 a month into an investment over 30 years.

Dollar Cost Averaging is especially important for young investors. A $10 a month investment starting at the age of eight can yield huge returns in 60 years.

When I was 25 years old and fresh off the pro tennis tour, I asked a financial advisor with Merrill Lynch if she would work with me. I had a whopping $2,500 to my name. She said her minimum was $10,000 but asked if I was willing to Dollar Cost Average every month. I didn't even know what that meant, but I said yes. She asked if I could make a monthly commitment of $100. Financial advisors make an average of 100 basis points or a 1% fee of assets under management.

She knew that if I Dollar Cost Averaged $100 every month, she would make a sizable 1% fee income from me in just a few years.

But even if you are 60 years old, Dollar Cost Averaging still works. Try contributing a few hundred dollars to your retirement portfolio every month. The real secret in the sauce is whether you can stay disciplined.

Chances are you will start out well, but fall soon to bad financial habits. Many financial institutions can automatically deduct a Dollar Cost Averaging payment from your paycheck. They will usually set it up for free.

You probably already know about this from mortgage and car payments. Often because of procrastination, payments are late. But the institution will usually offer a 25 basis point discount if you let them deduct the payment from your bank account.

Market Timing

All of us hear stories about people who have made perfect investment decisions at the perfect time. They sold their investments right before a market collapse, and bought at the very bottom. For every one person who gets lucky, a thousand lose. As I discussed earlier, if you missed the six best days in the stock market over the last year, your returns would lag 4% below the S&P or Dow Jones index.

I was at my brother Kevin's house Thanksgiving of 2008. I had already lost 40% of my investment portfolio.

My brother bragged that he sold most of his investments a year earlier. I was so jealous of his great luck, that I keep asking how he knew. I never got a firm answer, although I was happy for his great fortune.

One very famous economist, Harry Dent, was rumored to have sold his house in Florida in 2007 at the perfect time before the real estate market collapse.

But curiously, he was only willing to sell to those who would let him rent back as a condition of the sale. Either he was lucky or one of most brilliant people in America, but he leased his own house back from 2007 until 2010. And then bought his house at a discount when the real estate market was at the bottom. It's a great story, but don't try this on your own. It's better to stay invested then to take this kind of risk.

One of my tennis buddies, Barney, was a day trader.

Over a couple of beers, I asked inappropriately how much he made. I think I never got him drunk enough for much candor. He said his goal was to make money every day, no matter how much or how little. But the truth is, day traders rarely make money. Warm Buffett once said on a play from Sir Isaac Newton's laws of motion, "For investors as a whole, returns decrease as motion increases." Aside from commissions, the more you trade, the greater your chances for low returns.

Often day traders react to recent news. Most professional traders say, "buy the rumor, sell the news."

But Nobel laureate, Daniel Kahneman, once said that we have a tendency to react to recent news. He said we are guided by the immediate emotional impact of gains and losses, not by the long-term prospects of wealth.

How to Pick a Financial Advisor

I speak to many, many investor groups on my book, "Why Smart People Make Dumb Mistakes with their Money." I'm often asked if I do financial planning. The truth of the matter is, that I'm a writer, researcher, and coach, not a financial advisor. In 1981, I worked for the boutique Wall Street investment banking company called Kidder Peabody. The joke was, I cold called 150 times per day, and got rejected 149 times per day, with one call a day to my mother. After three months, even my mother said, "Don't call me again." I had a PhD, but no real world experience. But as a stock broker, I got to know what made a great financial advisor.

There are several kinds of financial advisors currently.

One with a CFP, or Certified Financial Advisor designation. Another popular advisor has a series 65 license and is called a Registered Investment Advisor.

The last is an insurance agent licensed to sell securities.

The real difference between the three, is the CFP is likely to sell you illiquid investments and use active money management. Assets Under Management or AUM would give them a 1% fee. They might also sell variable annuities, which can increase or decrease in value based on the investments in the underlying annuity subaccounts. What this all means is that CFP's have a distinctive investment philosophy.

The Registered Investment Advisors, or RIA's, make their money mainly from fees charged for Assets Under management. These fees can range from 1% to 3%, depending on the size of your portfolio. Often RIA's will sell you investment products in addition.

These could be real estate investment trusts, oil and gas partnerships, or any other investment that seems appropriate. While

RIA's and CFP's are closely related, there is a fiduciary and suitability regulatory standard.

Many investment advisors only need the investment to be suitable. This basically means that it's suitable for you and your portfolio depending on your needs. Fiduciary Standard means it's the best investment for you and your financial goals. RIA's have this Fiduciary Standard while the rest often are held to suitability.

While there is a difference between RIA's, many will put your portfolio into the stock market through Assets Under Management or actively manage your portfolio. They will gather assets, giving your money to a third-party company that rebalances your portfolio based on your risk tolerance.

Many RIA's are also from the insurance industry.

They are likely to put the safe portion of your investments into fixed indexed annuities. These are annuities that are guaranteed not to decrease in value yet mirror the stock market but at a decreased return. This is how the insurance companies are able to make sure that you don't take losses. These annuities also have a holding period often of seven years. If you want to liquidate the annuity before the seventh-year, there's often a sizable surrender charge. You should always ask about surrender charges on any annuity you consider. Another question you probably should ask, is the background of the financial advisor. If they came from the insurance industry, they probably believe in fixed indexed annuities.

The Certified Financial Advisors or CFP's are different.

They will often use active money management strategies. But part of their safe money focus, are variable annuities. These types of annuities can lose money or make money depending on the stock market return.

The CFP's tend not to sell fixed indexed annuities saying they are too expensive for the investor.

While the CFP designation training tends to be more rigorous, the RIA designation testing is difficult also. Another category is the Certified Investment Management Advisor designation, CIMA. These advisors tend to work with more high net worth accredited investors with more than $1 million in investment assets.

The question you need to ask every financial advisor or broker is 1, what are their fees and how do they get paid. Number 2, how often will they communicate with you by telephone or face-to-face. And number 3 whether you are an A, B, or C client. An A client will probably have more than $1 million in investable assets and often is a professional or business owner 50 years or older. A "B" client often has investment assets of more than $500,000 and is an upcoming professional or business owner over the age of 40. A "C" client is often anyone below $500,000 with no real prospects of adding to that portfolio.

The reason this is important to you as an investor is service. An A client is usually contacted by the advisor every month or two. They are often invited to events, and get much more attention from the advisor for accounting, estate planning, and insurance issues.

A "B" client is also valuable to the advisor. But they are unlikely to be contacted by the advisor more than two times per year. The advisor probably will not be as attentive to accounting, estate planning and insurance questions. The "C" client category gets the least attention. Most advisors will do a face-to-face review with you once a year. Aside from a monthly newsletter, that's the most attention you will get. Many larger financial planning firms will give their "C" clients to junior financial advisors with very little experience. My personal opinion is that you should look for a financial advisor who will talk to you once every three months, on the telephone or face-to-face. The advisor should also talk to your accountant and other relevant advisors annually. And lastly, be willing to rebalance your portfolio every quarter. If it takes a smaller firm to give you that kind of service, then so be it. Financial planning is more about the relationship than investment perfection.

In 2008, most investment planning firms lost clients. This was not because they lost money, but they failed to communicate with their clients. They feared that calling clients with bad news would cause the clients to leave. Actually the opposite happened. Not talking to their clients made them leave. In fact 82% of clients in 2008 warned their family and friends away from their own financial advisors, because of lack of contact. Today 75% of clients over the age of 55 are postponing retirement or going back to work to augment their income. Nearly all of this stems from poor client contact. So make sure that you do your due diligence and get a commitment from a financial advisor of what they will provide if you invest your money through their firm.

Also check out the financial advisors' complaint record. When a complaint or sanction has been logged against a financial advisor, it will be reflected in their U4 report. You may want to ask the advisor directly what complaints they have on their U4. Most will tell you with an explanation. Not every U4 complaint has merit. One of my coaching clients had a complaint lodged by a long time financial planning client. The client complained they never knew an annuity they bought had a surrender period of seven years, even though they signed the application and disclosure. The broker-dealer supervising the financial advisor decided that legal fees required to fight the allegation were not worth it and settled with the client. Even though the client was in the wrong. The compromise settlement ended in a ding on the advisors U4.

The bottom line is you should pick a financial advisor who will make you an "A" or "B" client, call you every three months, discloses their fees and commissions, and show you their U4 report. Beyond that, make sure they are somebody you can communicate with easily, and trust over the long-term. I think you know by now, investing on your own is much more risky and will cost you more money in lost investment returns than the commissions and fees you will pay to a financial advisor.

The downside is since you have made it this far in Why Smart People Make Dumb Mistakes With Their Money, you probably know more now than most professional advisors do about investor behavior. You may have to educate them on what you know. But that will only help you build a better relationship with your financial planner.

So now you have learned your own emotions have more impact on your money decisions than your own common sense. You have also learned there is hope.

You can make good decisions about your investments and the way you earn and spend money. But it is up to you to make the changes necessary to improve. Not many people can change. But my bet is you can do it.

Please let me know at Kerry@kerryjohnson.com. I want to hear about how you have applied the techniques we have discussed.